D0934117

To Eugene and Jean Bay...

I'm pleased to present you with a copy of this book so you can see how spontaneous and natural mentoring works in a person's life. Jesus is the greatest mentor of all times (and let's not forget Barnabas who mentored Mark).

Built to Help Each Other

You will enjoy reading this book for its humor and the remarkable stories of Richard Caruso's life, which led him to be named the Entrepreneur of the Year of the United States of America. It will cause you to reflect on who mentored you, and those you have mentored — your BMPC family, friends, and others.

In friendship & Christian love,

John Llobsby

March 15, 2021

Built to Help Each Other

MENTORING IN THE LIFE OF
RICHARD CARUSO: AN UNCOMMON MAN

John Crosby
with Richard Caruso

We humans are built to help each other.
—Richard E. Caruso, PhD

RADIUS BOOK GROUP
NEW YORK

Distributed by Radius Book Group
A division of Diversion Publishing Corp.
443 Park Avenue South, Suite 1004
New York, NY 10016
www.RadiusBookGroup.com

Copyright © 2019 by John C. Crosby

All rights reserved, including the right to reproduce this book or portions thereof in any form whatsoever. No part of this publication may be reproduced or transmitted in any form or by any means, electronic or mechanical, including photocopying, recording, or any other information storage and retrieval, without the written permission of the author.

For more information, e-mail info@radiusbookgroup.com.

First edition: June 2019
Hardcover ISBN: 978-1-63576-642-4
Trade Paperback ISBN: 978-1-63576-644-8
eBook ISBN: 978-1-63576-708-7

Library of Congress Control Number: 2018965571

Manufactured in the United States of America

10 9 8 7 6 5 4 3 2 1

Cover design by Charles Hames
Interior design by Scribe Inc.

Radius Book Group and the Radius Book Group colophon are registered trademarks of Radius Book Group, a division of Diversion Publishing Corp.

To Sally Feitig Caruso and Frances Caruso Holtz,
whose interest and passion for this book exceeded all others,
and
the Caruso Family

IN MEMORIAM
Cono Sarafino Caruso
1893–1985

Louise Pirolli Caruso
1902–1978

CONTENTS

Acknowledgments   ix
John Crosby

Introduction   1
Richard Caruso

1   Finding a Way—Italy to 1961   3
2   A Vision of What's Possible—1961 to 1966   17
3   Supporting the Old While Starting
    the New—1966 to 1977   29
4   Growing a Company; Growing a Family—
    1977 to 1986   43
5   Making Mentoring Mainstream—1986 to 1988   63
6   Stepping Back to Go Forward—1988 to 1990   83
7   Falling Seven, Rising Eight—1990 to 1996   93
8   Regeneration—1996 to 2015   111
9   Coda   129

Afterword: UIF Today—2015 and Beyond   141
Appendix 1: Richard Caruso's Nine Goals   167
Appendix 2: Ten Steps for Establishing a Corporate
            (Structured) Mentoring Program   169
Appendix 3: Richard Caruso's Three Systems
            of Mentoring   171

CONTENTS

Appendix 4: Inspirational Mentoring Resources   183

Appendix 5: The Failed Experiment—
        John Burke and Ioannis Yannas   189

A List of Recommended Books   195

Index   199

ACKNOWLEDGMENTS

Richard Caruso has been my partner since we started the Uncommon Individual Foundation (UIF) in 1986. I owe him an enormous debt of gratitude for making that phone call asking me to make this amazing journey with him of creating the first non-profit foundation devoted exclusively to mentoring. In his words, "Let's do for others what others have done for us." Rich fulfilled this goal with the passion and perseverance he's shown since child-hood, believing that hard work and a never-give-up attitude was the way to do the impossible.

In 2013, Richard began writing about his life to inspire others to foster these same characteristics, but in 2014, the brain that had never failed him began to falter. He would ask me, "John, are you having trouble with your brain? Strange things are happen-ing to mine." By 2015, with the capable help of Jessica Stokes, an English major at Penn, and writer Helen Green, he had written seventy-four pages about his business success. In 2017, seeing the draft gathering dust, I vowed to finish it. It's a story that needs to be told. It's a life that needs to be shared with his family, friends, colleagues, and the world interested in mentoring.

My deepest thanks goes to my writing partner and editor, Joanna Carnahan, who was able to bring to life how multiple men-tors influenced Richard's life as well as mine. She set aside other priorities and put in days, nights, and weekends with complete dedication to find the best way to illuminate the power that mentoring can have on anyone's life.

Together, in this book, Joanna and I share the groundbreaking research of Richard's closed and open systems of mentoring first reported in his PhD dissertation at the London School of Economics in 1990. This cutting-edge philosophy states that traditional one-on-one mentoring works but that multiple mentoring can often be more powerful. Rich turned everyone who could help him into a sometime mentor and used other resources, such as books, articles, inspirational quotes, art, and poetry to mentor him as well. He proved that these resources can often be more influential than an assigned mentor.

This book could not have included its humor and personal memories without Richard's family: his wife, Sally, and two sons, Jonathan and Peter; brothers, Carmen and Joe; sister, Frances Caruso Holtz; nephews, Jerry and David Holtz; and nieces, Dana Holtz Conner, Bonnie Caruso Anido, and Kristin Caruso Clark. I am grateful to Jeff and Pat Robbins for introducing me to Richard's horse-racing partnership and his delight in seeing his horses both win and lose at the race track in Philadelphia. Italo Manzi shared his experience in helping Richard build the beautiful addition to his Villanova home, which led to a lifelong friendship and to his fulltime management of Richard's impressive real estate holdings.

College roommates John Pignatore and Bill Muir provided insight to Richard's character and have remained friends with him over the years. Mary Muolo at Susquehanna University was always available to provide Rich's football honors and essential information from his college years. Much appreciation goes to Henry Haines, who was Richard's roommate after he graduated college, and Herb Brown, who worked closely with Rich in the early days at Lease Financing Corporation. I am also grateful to have located Peter Tyrrell and Ronnie Wagenhein, who grew up with Richard and went to school with him in Atlantic City. Their memories added spice to the story of young Richie's life, revealing telling shenanigans that might otherwise have been lost forever.

Jerry Holtz and Gary DiLella were indispensable in writing this book. Although Richard didn't give titles to his staff at the Provco Group, believing all work there is a team effort (just as it was on his Susquehanna football team), I bestow the title of CEO on Jerry and CFO on Gary. Both have worked intimately with Rich and been involved day in and day out with making impeccable decisions. They provided me timelines, fact checks, and stories of Rich's exceptional business and human qualities. I also want to shed light on a Provco accountant, Kathleen Crenny, who has the heart and soul of an angel, lighting Richard's life with her unlimited support and caregiving. Pam Urbas, an expert in yoga and meditation, shared her knowledge and support as Richard relentlessly fights on with an intense mental focus. Other caregivers one cannot overlook are Provco's devoted staff and Richard's sons, Jonathan and Peter, who spend time with their dad every day.

Jim Sullivan shared his experience of working with Richard in the early 1980s on one of the first large entrepreneurial deals, buying and selling the Rustler Steak House Chain. Jim was invaluable in helping me tell the story of how this led to a lifelong friendship and a seat on Integra's board of trustees. At the London School of Economics, Richard's doctoral advisor was Keith Bradley, who now serves on Integra's board. Talking long distance from London, Dr. Bradley informed me of the impact that Richard's innovative research has had on the phenomenon of mentoring.

Stuart Essig, board chair and former CEO of Integra Life-Sciences, generously gave his time to talk about his long friendship with Richard and how Rich influenced the inconceivable success of Integra, making it the leading regenerative tissue technology and neurosurgery company in the world. Judi O'Grady, whom Rich brought from a Marion Merrell Dow Company in Kansas City, could not have been more accommodating with her time. She provided technical editing and sent me pages of emails about the history of Integra. She rose to be corporate vice president of global regulatory affairs, completing approximately forty-five acquisitions of companies and product lines that improve the quality of life for thousands of patients throughout the world.

The staff at the Uncommon Individual Foundation has been enormously helpful: managing directors Joe Lopez and Michael Hackman; together with Ben Pietrzyk and Andrew Zivic, who began as interns from La Salle and Villanova, respectively; Chris DiAntonio and Jon Rodriquez; Lucy Lopez and Jake Smolinski; Betsy Dwyer; Christine Heard; and Shakia Kirksey. I thank these incredible team members, together with UIF's affiliated entrepreneurs and college and high school associate interns, for their passion and commitment to the foundation's mission and goals.

Mark Fretz and Evan Phail at Radius Book Group and Naomi Gunkel at Scribe Inc. were truly exceptional and remarkably patient with me in every aspect of this bookmaking process. As a novice, I depended on their expert guidance, advice, support, and attention to detail. Thank you, Charles Hames, for the handsome cover design after patiently tolerating my persnickety ideas.

I am especially grateful to my wife, Marlene, who jumped in with pencil in hand to participate in all personal interviews and phone calls, writing and typing notes, collecting pictures, and making suggestions on topics, chapter titles, and quotes. She read every draft of each chapter multiple times. Her dedication and passion for this project—as well as her enthusiasm and support—were truly inspiring. When I shared my personal stories, I heard her voice in my head reminding me to speak from the heart with the power of being vulnerable and authentic. She is my closest advisor and the love of my life, supporting me every step of the way with great insight and love.

John C. Crosby, EdD
June 2019

INTRODUCTION

I learned to use imagination and creativity to find my own way.
—RICHARD E. CARUSO

*I*mpossible is not a word in my dictionary. When it's judged that something I want to achieve can't be accomplished, I feel even more motivated to take on the project and work to transform my goals into reality.

From a young age, I faced obstacles that came with being born into a large, working-class, Italian-American family in Atlantic City, New Jersey. Both of my parents came to the United States from Italy as children, found each other years later, and created our family. It was an unlikely start for achieving what follows.

In those early years, I had no idea where my aspirations might lead. Two threads stand out as constants, though: a strong faith and natural mentoring. Now they seem to me the main reason I was able to achieve the "impossible."

In 2015, the National Italian American Foundation gave me its Special Achievement Award in Business for work with Integra LifeSciences Corporation. Nearly twenty years earlier, I'd founded Integra on the notion that the human body might be able to regenerate skin tissue even when it had been badly burned or compromised through injury. Others had attempted for years to bring to market Artificial Skin Integra™ and had given up. Many said it couldn't be done.

As a first-generation American, I was blessed with parents who didn't hold back my aspirations with their expectations. They allowed me to struggle, dream, and build a life of my own design. I was free to exercise the entrepreneurial spirit that seems to have always been part of me.

That spirit has led to satisfaction, success, and eventually accolades, which have felt supremely gratifying. Every one of those professional successes, though, involved collaboration with other like-minded, supportive individuals. Without their help and encouragement, if they hadn't shared their knowledge and energy, my life would have been very different.

We didn't use the word then, but it has become clear that they were *mentors* to me. They helped me grow into who I am, and from that understanding, I've learned one essential lesson: the power of mentoring can release the Uncommon Individual within anyone.

Now using my own story to share insights into mentoring, I hope to provide inspiration and encouragement to others.

Richard E. Caruso, PhD
November 2015

CHAPTER 1

FINDING A WAY

ITALY TO 1961

*He was very proud of where he grew up and the house
where he lived in Atlantic City. He took me by his
house several times and was proud of his Italian heritage.*
—HERB BROWN

When she was a little girl, Maria Louisa Pirolli's father died in Venafro, a mountainous area near Pompeii and Naples. Soon after, in 1911, Louisa's mother left Italy for the United States, taking two of her sons and nine-year-old Louisa. In Philadelphia, they focused on supporting themselves. Everyone helped, but Louisa got to go to school, took *Louise* as her American name, and learned to speak English fluently.

Around the same time, teenage Cono Caruso left Capo d'Orlando, in Sicily. He traveled by himself to the United States to live with a family friend and work, picking up his new language well enough to make a living. For the rest of his long life, he understood English better than he could speak it.

Also for the rest of his life he saved. He saved for years to buy his own house. Then the stock market crashed. His bank closed. He lost everything he'd saved.

So . . . Cono kept on working—as a waiter for Atlantic City hotels (the Claridge, Hotel Dennis, Chelsea Hotel, the Traymore) and as a carpenter when he could find repair jobs. He adapted to the guys at work sometimes calling him Nick or Nicholas, and he found a way to make a living from what life offered.

After mutual friends introduced them, he also found time to see Louise. Cono was forty-one when they married on April 29, 1935, barely a week before Louise's thirty-third birthday, and then moved into the little house in Atlantic City that Cono had finally saved enough to buy: 2314 Leopold Terrace.

It's where their first child, a son, was born, and then died from complications during birth.

Their son Carmen came in April 1938; a daughter, Frances, in September 1939; Richard Ernest Joseph on May 12, 1943; and Joseph in March 1947, nearly two years after his mother had become a US citizen.

To their growing-up-American children, Louise and Cono spoke only English. To each other, they spoke Italian.

Louise found room for each new child in their small home. Rich ("Ree," his mother called him) shared a room with his older brother Carmen. That put an extra set of eyes on Rich and gave him an extra layer of protection. As they grew, Carmen had trouble sleeping because Rich, by age seven or eight, had begun snoring—sometimes so loud that Carmen threw a pillow over Rich's face to stop the noise. It did occur to Carmen, though, that the pillow might stop Rich's breathing too, so he finally told their parents. They took Rich to a doctor who said tonsils were the problem and had them taken out.

Around that time, a man came to their front door selling live chickens, and Rich saw his father buy one. Cono put the chicken in the basement, and soon Rich went down to see it. The next afternoon, he went down to visit the chicken again, but it was gone. Then Rich realized they'd had chicken for dinner the night before. He wouldn't eat chicken for another ten years, and his family took note—of his soft heart and of his determination.

During his children's growing-up years, Cono, of course, kept right on working—to pay for chickens, medical bills, and everything else they had to get from other people. He wasn't home much. When he worked at the Seaview Country Club in Galloway Township, ten miles north of Atlantic City, he had to take three buses to get there—he never learned to drive; he never owned a car.

Louise kept right on working too, from home, even growing some of their own food in their tiny garden—and flowers, always flowers—providing all she could so they needed less, so Cono's wages would be enough.

Two parents at home every night, their own house, enough food, enough clothes, church, school, neighbors: it was more than many children had. Louise and Cono worked hard to keep all those pieces in place. Much later, Rich put it simply: "My parents were struggling to support our family, and so they had little time to spend with us."

Rich saw that downside and came to accept it. By 1st or 2nd grade, he was noticing something like an upside too. All four children walked to the nearby grammar school that was part of their church, St. Michael's. One day Rich's religion teacher asked him if he'd help the priests with mass and communion on Sundays, as an altar boy. He thought about it a bit and then said yes, feeling no need to ask his parents first.

Later, he remembered this as the first time he'd taken the initiative to make that big a decision by himself. He saw it as a turning point: "Undertaking the enterprise of my own life," he'd call it.

As an adult, he'd believe that every choice each of us makes, every action we take, shapes our brains, our future, our selves. He'd say that all of us are born with the freedom we need to develop ourselves.

He'd describe Louise and Cono as supportive: "They never told me not to fail or not to take risks; and because I had few restrictions, I was forced to discover who I was and what I wanted to do on my own." He remembered thinking, even at around six years old, that he and his siblings were responsible for developing their own lives and futures.

So develop he did.

When Rich was in 4th grade, every weekday as he left for school, Louise gave him twenty-five cents—what it cost to buy the least expensive lunch at school, but half the price of the nearby White House Sub Shop's delicious hoagie, so famous that Frank Sinatra came by to get one now and then. One day Rich discovered a store near school with a pinball machine that cost a quarter to play. If you won the game, you won fifty cents, enough to buy the hoagie. However, if you lost the game, you lost your quarter—which meant, for Rich, no lunch. Rich decided to try it and played almost every day. He went during lunch without his friends "because I didn't want them to know that my family didn't have much money." As a grown-up, he remembered winning the game—and getting lunch—75 percent of the time, and he remembered savoring each bite of that hoagie every time he won: "The bread had just the right crunch on the outside but was doughy and soft on the inside." Most of all, though, he remembered how good he felt about figuring out a way to get those hoagies all by himself.

Still, that summer when an ice cream truck began driving by his house, Rich's first strategy was to run and ask his parents for money. "We don't have any extra money for ice cream," they answered every time, until Rich finally stopped asking them and began asking himself.

Their house was near the Atlantic City Convention Center, and all day long there were people walking on the boardwalk in front of it. Rich decided to start his first business right outside the convention center shining shoes: "In our house I found some half-used tins of polish in different colors, a frayed horsehair brush, and a greasy shine cloth that my dad had used for his own shoes. I took these to the boardwalk and polished the shoes of men on their way to work, lunch meetings, and conferences."

It worked so well that by the next summer, before 6th grade, he felt confident enough to try something new. His second business plan went like this: "The beach was a block and a half from our house. Big daily newspapers put out two editions then, and I thought that by afternoon, vacationers who'd been on the beach all morning would want to know the latest news. I had dozens of copies of a large Philadelphia paper's afternoon edition delivered to our house and took them out to the beach to sell."

When Rich noticed that the boardwalk and beach were starting to empty for the day, he'd walk home, relishing the choice ahead: vanilla or chocolate. Anticipating that first lick, he'd look forward to what for him became the best part: buying ice cream for his friends.

The basic threads of Rich's life seemed to already be in place by age eleven: belonging within a family and a faith, feeling free to want more and reach for it, knowing it was up to him to get what he wanted and believing he could, looking around for opportunities, searching out resources to tap, taking definite steps and seeing which worked, and even learning by then how good it feels to share with others.

"I was learning to create a business plan based on a personal dream" was how he'd put it much later. "I never had anything handed to me, so I learned to use imagination and creativity to find my own way. When those ways worked, as shining shoes and selling papers did, I felt an incredible sense of independence and empowerment. Some of my tries failed, though. That felt worse at first but turned out to be important because it helped me realize that there's no such thing as success without failure. Working on my own to get what I wanted, succeeding and failing, helped me develop a resilience that's been invaluable throughout life."

Of course, some dreams took longer to realize than others. When Rich was eight or nine, he saw a stray dog at school and asked his mother if he could bring it home to live with them. She'd said no. Persisting, he'd taken scraps of bread, cheese, or meat to school and fed the dog, so the dog followed him home each afternoon. "I can't help it, Mama. He just likes me," Rich would claim, but there really wasn't enough room for a dog.

All six of them—Cono, Louise, Carmen, Fran, Rich, and Joe—overfilled the little house that Cono had saved twice for . . . until the summer of 1955, right before Rich was to begin 7th grade. That's when Cono, who'd kept on working and saving, bought a larger house for them: 102 North Kenyon Avenue, four miles away in Margate.

By then the family had seen Rich adopting his parents' strong work ethic. They'd also seen evidence of his big heart, trying to save animals and using his own earnings to buy treats for friends. Both were traits to be proud of in their twelve-year-old. Had he picked up his father's saving habit too, or had he spent all his profits on ice cream?

"Before we moved into the new home," Rich remembered, "I came across an ad in the classifieds of a local paper: *DOG FOR SALE*. I contacted the seller and told him I wanted to buy the dog. A few days later, he came to drop her off at our house, and I paid for her with my own money. I hadn't told my family about buying the dog, so all of them were surprised when I walked through the front door with the new pet. We moved a few weeks later to our Margate home and brought my first dog with us." Rich had indeed learned to save.

With those savings, he also bought a camera, which wasn't accepted by the family as readily as the dog had been. No one minded that he'd bought himself this new gadget until he started taking pictures of them. Most of the family posed for him a time or two and then ignored him, but not his dad. For some reason Cono did *not* want his picture taken, and for some reason Rich *especially* wanted to photograph his father. As Cono's "no's" got louder, Rich clicked more. One time, a furious Cono chased after his independent son, who laughed as he kept turning around and snapping more photos of his dad while running away from him.

Later, as adults, his family laughed too when they looked at these pictures and retold the story. They also remembered that old-school, authoritarian part of their father. He could be very strict, and he didn't laugh at this bid for his attention. The way he saw it, his job was to provide for them, and they were to do as they were told.

That wasn't the way Rich wanted it, but already one of his best-developed strengths was making good use of whatever he had. For the rest of his life, he worked at maintaining a relationship with his dad that worked for both of them.

Also for the rest of his life, Rich worked on developing connections with others. That was a particularly useful skill about then because his circle of friends was about to expand. Blessed Sacrament, the new Catholic elementary school in Margate, was growing by adding one grade a year, opening its 2nd grade that fall. The youngest Caruso, Joseph, was enrolled there. Margate's public Granville Avenue School went through 8th grade, but Rich wanted to be with friends at St. Michael's for 7th and 8th grades, so he rode the city bus to get there. Soon, though, he began thinking of the four-mile rides as burdensome. Before Thanksgiving, he'd transferred to the public school in Margate.

He made new friends there. One of them, Peter Tyrrell, saw other Margate students tease Rich, calling him by his middle name, Ernest, when he'd ask the teacher after school to explain something new until he understood it well. Rich was curious—he wanted to know *how* and *why*. Such digging deep became characteristic for him—so did figuring out ways to handle teasing and bullying.

Another friend from junior high gave Rich the bridge to a life he hadn't imagined as possible before then: "After graduating from 8th grade, I transferred to Atlantic City High School. There was a Catholic high school in the area, but I decided to go to the public school because that's where most of my friends, from both St. Michael's and Margate, were going." One of those friends was David Aiken: "David had wonderful parents and an amazing house in Margate where we spent a great deal of time together. He loved football, introduced me to the game, and I got very interested in it. We both tried out for the football team as freshmen and made it. We trained together almost every day, at every scheduled football practice, of course, and often at home too." David's home gave Rich a feel for a different life, and football became part of a path to that life—but it wasn't a direct road by any means.

Rich was not attending classes "almost every day." He and several of his other friends skipped frequently.

Ronnie Wagenhein, whom Rich had met in 7th grade, remembered that "sometimes Rich took off from school on Friday afternoons and met with Alan (Pencil) Cohen, the nephew of Paul (Skinny) D'Amato, whose popular 500 Club was a block away from the Caruso house. Skinny was known as 'Mr. Atlantic City,' and the club allegedly was a front for an illegal gambling operation. To draw gamblers, Skinny had big-name entertainers such as his friend Frank Sinatra, Sammy Davis Jr., and other stars of the time perform at the club. Pencil got his nickname because sometimes in fights he'd try to poke the other guy in the eye with a pencil. Once, Rich and Pencil stole some hubcaps to make money."

That didn't fit with Rich's altar-boy ethics, but it was hard making all your own spending money. Besides, being tough was the only way Rich knew to handle the bullies, who seemed to be everywhere—he was *not* going to be bullied. Plus, the school subjects "weren't interesting," Rich would say; but there was a deeper reason. He'd heard that college tuition cost a lot of money, and he knew his parents couldn't pay for it. Why bother?

His successful, grown-up self remembered that time in a calm, rational way: "A number of my friends had already quit school to get jobs, and that fall I considered doing the same, planning to open a car-body repair shop. This seemed a reasonable plan for my future because I had an interest in, and skill for, fixing cars. Even then, before being old enough to drive, I'd buy old junk cars with money I'd earned and repair them for fun. I'd just always assumed that even if I did graduate from high school, I wouldn't attend college. I stayed in school for the fall of my freshman year because of my love for football but was seriously considering dropping out after the season ended."

His older brother showed Rich a different path, though. The year Rich started 8th grade, Carmen graduated from Atlantic City High School and began college, paying his own tuition by working a part-time job in Philadelphia.

Rich got the idea that he might be able to do that too. Besides, his coaches were noticing him and encouraging him. So he stayed in school after football season ended, and then went back the next year, and then the next.

He even took a second look at some of those *uninteresting* subjects. Science, for example, could be kind of intriguing. By the end of his junior year, he'd been awarded a certificate from the New Jersey Science Teachers Association: "For Outstanding Scholarship in Science–General Physics."

As this different image of his future emerged, so did new enthusiasm. Rich got one or more business-related jobs every summer in high school, and he opened his own bank account. He liked seeing the balance grow and liked "the regular reminders of the benefits of hard work."

What he called his "first real job" was with a local soda manufacturing company. Common practice back then was for customers to buy soft drinks at soda fountains, where the drinks would usually be poured out of the bottle into glasses, over ice, and served, sometimes with a garnish. The store would return the empty bottles to the soda company to be reused.

As Rich explained it, "My job was to oversee manufacturing of the soda; clean, fill, and cap the recycled bottles; put the newly filled bottles into a crate; load the crates onto delivery trucks; and deliver the sodas to various businesses. Even though I was underage, I looked older, knew how to drive, and held this position several summers." In time, he even got a license to drive legally.

That job helped Rich grow up in several ways, one of which he remembered vividly. The delivery sheet said "Camp Sunshine," a place he hadn't been to before. When he drove up, the man who came to get the crate was wearing an apron and nothing else. That's when Rich learned there was such a thing as a nudist colony. Eventually, his family heard about that particular delivery and turned it into a story they'd tell, for years, to elicit from Rich a tiny, wry smile, if not the hint of a blush.

The summer before his senior year, he worked at a car repair shop and gas station and became friends with the owner. Merging work life and social life would become a pattern for Rich.

Peter Tyrrell became a close, lifelong friend from 7th grade on. Looking back on their school years, Peter especially remembered Rich working: "He worked hard at everything he did: football, other sports, and all his jobs. One summer, he worked on Black-horse Pike at a garage changing truck tires, sometimes until three o'clock in the morning. He took tires off rims and put new ones on: those large, semi-truck tires, back when you had to change a tire with a tire iron. It was hard work. It took strength. One time Rich also had a landscaping job that he'd work at from eight o'clock in the morning until dusk." Peter remembered Rich in those days as "well-educated and also street smart—a tough kid, ready to fight if a fight were called for." He wasn't the only one to use the words *smart* and *tough* to describe Rich.

Another of Rich's jobs was as an usher at the movie theater in Atlantic City. He'd watch the films over and over, at every showing, eventually memorizing every word. On Friday nights, Ronnie Wagenheim would sometimes meet Rich at the theater after work, and they'd go sit under the Ventnor pier and talk about life. Ronnie too was impressed with Rich's intelligence and toughness: "When Rich was fifteen or sixteen, he looked twenty-five and needed to shave a lot—we'd send him to the liquor store for us! Nobody messed with Rich; he was the toughest guy in school. Only one guy was able to hit him. Once that guy came to the movie theater, saw Rich sitting and cracked him in the face, ran as fast as he could out of the theater, and spent the rest of high school hiding from Rich."

Later, Rich remembered that during those summers, most of his friends spent time relaxing at the beach but that he was always working "at least one full-time job each summer, up to seven days a week." Decades later, he'd say that those jobs "helped me understand the business world and appreciate the value of personal responsibility." Also, the physical labor kept him in good shape for his last year of high school football.

That spring, as Rich had finished his junior year in high school, Carmen had graduated from college and been offered a full-time job. Rich was paying attention. He went back to school for his senior year. He'd graduate from high school. Maybe he'd try the path Carmen had taken, working his way through college. "My brother had a significant impact on my future," Rich later said. "Natural mentoring" was what he'd come to call Carmen's example.

"After football season had ended in my senior year," Rich recalled, "I was walking down the hall of the high school when my football coach, John Boyd, called out, 'Hey, Richie! Do you want to go to college? We have coaches here today waiting to interview football players.' I stopped and answered, 'Yes, Coach, I'd like to go to college.' I'd never heard of scholarships for athletes!" When David Aiken had introduced Rich to football in junior high, neither had guessed that it could be a path to college.

"Coach Boyd set up an appointment for me with one college coach that same day and with several others from various colleges on following days." One of them Boyd knew personally was Jim Garrett, the new head football coach at Susquehanna University. He'd played for the New York Giants, and his son Jason would coach the Dallas Cowboys someday, but Rich knew none of that then. The interview with Jim Garrett just stood out for Rich somehow.

"After our meeting, Coach Garrett developed a special interest in recruiting me, and I decided I wanted to visit Susquehanna before making any decisions. My sister, Fran, four years older, had a Volkswagen Beetle by then and told me she'd let me drive it the two-hundred-plus miles to Selinsgrove, Pennsylvania, where Susquehanna University was. I went up on a weekend, taking the 76-west highway. It was the first time I'd ever left New Jersey."

Years later, Rich remembered being fascinated on his drive up at seeing the high-speed highway with no median barriers, but when he got to the university, what impressed him most was how the students were dressed: "At Atlantic City High School, I was used to boys wearing bell-bottomed pants with wildly patterned shirts and girls wearing very short skirts with thick makeup on their faces, but at Susquehanna, students wore more understated clothing. The women wore very little makeup and dresses with full skirts, and the men were dressed in a way that seemed more professional to me. I assumed this more modest style of dress meant the students were more mature and responsible than those in my high school. From then on, I was very interested in attending Susquehanna."

Another draw was a man Rich met on that same visit, Bob Pittello: "I was impressed by his handsome suit as well as his Cadillac. At first I thought he was a professor." It turns out he was the assistant football coach.

As his senior year went on, Rich had interviews with and offers from other colleges, but by then he'd made up his mind: he wanted to be at Susquehanna and wanted to play football with Coach Garrett and Coach Pittello: "When they gave me an offer, I accepted, joining the roster of the Susquehanna Crusaders."

Both Coach Boyd and Coach Garrett helped Rich get the athletic scholarship he needed. For the rest of his life, he remembered what they did and the myriad ways they helped him, before and after this turning point. He came to see them in the bigger picture of his life and values: "These men were assigned to me as coaches but evolved into what I now see as natural mentors. Although coaching is a component of mentoring, coaching and mentoring serve two different purposes. Coaching focuses on development in specific areas, such as honing football skills. Mentoring focuses more on personal and professional development. My coaches did both. They truly helped shape my life."

Maybe they helped Rich because they valued helping *and* because they saw Rich's promise. Maybe he was able to make use of their help because of an inborn drive *and* because he'd been given a good enough base: the safety of a stable family balanced with freedom to reach for what he wanted and solve problems for himself. He'd copied the habits of hard work and patient saving his parents modeled, learned to cobble together hiding-in-plain-sight resources to reach personal goals, discovered that "failing" with one strategy just meant he had to try another, come to feel confident in his own abilities, and recognized the fun of teamwork and the fun of helping others. All that had led him to a beginning understanding of how life was shaped by both help from others *and* what he did with that help.

Those seemed like pretty good credentials to have for starting college.

CHAPTER 2

A VISION OF WHAT'S POSSIBLE
1961 TO 1966

*Successful people turn everyone who
can help them into a sometime mentor.*
—JOHN C. CROSBY

The number on Rich's football jersey at Susquehanna University was 64. That fall of 1961, he moved into a dorm, reconnected with Coach Garrett and Coach Pittello, and began practice. He wasn't a starter, but he and one other freshman got some playing time during every game that season. Rich played both offensive and defensive positions. He enjoyed his first semester in college.

Then, on March 6, 1962, the Ash Wednesday Storm hit the US East Coast. For three days, it pounded beaches, homes, and boardwalks along the New Jersey shoreline, including Atlantic City, Margate, and Ventnor. It was one of the worst storms to ever hit the state, and it soon converged with one of the worst events in Rich's life so far, to provide him with one of his hardest life lessons.

He got kicked out of school.

What must have seemed worse at first is that the decision was made by his fellow students: the Men's Judiciary Board, newly formed in response to the student body's push for the power to make such disciplinary decisions. "You are suspended from

Susquehanna University for the remainder of this semester for undesirable conduct," is how the dean of students put it in his letter to Rich and his parents on April 12, 1962.

As free as Rich had felt as a child, his parents saw that he was home every night; his teachers tracked his attendance at school; and his bosses, at one or two or three jobs, oversaw almost every other hour of his days. The freedom of college was a new, exhilarating time to experiment—or maybe do some wild and crazy things, and Rich did.

Once, when a group of freshman girls was near the men's dorm, Rich and three friends tried the then-popular prank of "mooning" them. It likely would have been just a slap-on-the-wrist infraction at US colleges fifty years later, but not at quiet Susquehanna in 1962.

However, the dean's letter was followed by two others that put a different slant on the incident. While students in the South were protesting during the civil rights movement, students on Susquehanna's campus were signing a petition protesting the suspensions of Rich and his friends. Some even sent his parents a letter that must have added pride to their mix of feelings: "A great percentage of Rich's fellow students are deeply disappointed in the decision that was made by the Men's Judiciary Board. . . . You have raised your son to be a gentleman. In school, he is respected and well-liked by all who know him. Also, he is well-mannered and sincere. Regardless of the decision, your son is still admired by his contemporaries for his qualities. *We want your son back with us in September.* He is the type of man that one remembers. We will stick by him; we hope that you will too." The letter was signed by 166 students, about half of them female.

Coach Garrett too, with the intuitive insight of a mentor, wrote to Cono and Louise: "I definitely would like to tell you very strongly that this incident is only a prank, a prank that has gotten out of hand. . . . I have not taken them to task and I do not feel harshly toward them. I believe strongly that this is the time that all friends, relatives, and interested people should rally around the boy and help him over this most difficult hurdle. He needs friends, encouragement, and genuine interest—not a lot of criticism and harsh words."

After reading these two letters, did Louise and Cono heed the advice? Did they see it as an error in their son's judgment but a lesson learned better now than later? Did they sense he felt humiliated and needed support, not criticism? Did they wonder if, years later, they'd all laugh about it?

Rich never talked about what his parents said to him when he returned to Margate from the college he'd gotten into against all odds. His own feelings ranged from embarrassed and discouraged, to angry, and eventually to determined. At first, he did see this as a personal disaster, mirrored by the physical wreckage all around him. Soon, however, as was coming to seem characteristic of Rich, he saw an upside too: the opportunity to do work that was needed, that he knew how to do, and that would give him very welcome income. Work would give him the dignity of being useful as well as time to figure out how to make up for the classes he couldn't finish this semester.

Strangely, the timing was perfect. As soon as he got home, Rich saw that "a massive repair effort was begun to rebuild or repair sand dunes, homes, boardwalks, and businesses devastated by this terrible storm. I was hired by a company to repair or replace damaged boardwalks along the beaches and soon after starting was promoted to a senior position on the team."

The boss saw right away that Rich had done construction before and that he often kept working when others were taking a break. Someone else was watching too—a man who owned a house in Ventnor right next to where Rich's crew was repairing the boardwalk.

One day the man walked over to the construction site and asked, "Who's that young man, the only one working, driving foundation piles in the sand?" A member of the crew replied, "Oh, that's Richie Caruso."

"Well, ask him to come over here when he's finished," said the man. "I want to talk with him."

When Rich came over later, the man introduced himself as Russell Baum. Would Rich be interested in helping him fix up his damaged vacation house? Rich would.

Almost every evening that spring, after finishing his day job on the boardwalk, Rich worked with Mr. Baum—and as they worked, they talked: "While we worked together, Mr. Baum asked me about what I'd done, what I wanted to do. Sometimes we kept talking even after we'd finished work for the day. He found out I was a football player and proceeded to connect me with West Point Military Academy and the US Naval Academy, both of which were interested in recruiting me."

One day that summer, Rich's brother Joseph—now called Joe and turning fifteen—was at home in Margate when Rich was, and the phone rang. It was for Rich. Joe Bellino, a Heisman Trophy winner who played for the Naval Academy, was "trying to entice Rich to go to Navy," as Joe Caruso remembered it. That had to have impressed both brothers, but Rich took his time: "After thinking about it for a while, I decided to return to Susquehanna: I felt the need for flexibility with my education and career path, and a military school didn't feel like a good fit."

In time, Rich learned that Russell Baum had been highly successful in selling manufacturing equipment and services up and down the East Coast for the Liberty Folding Company. Then in

1950, he'd bought the company, renaming it the Baumfolder Corporation. It had thrived under him during the past decade and would do so for three more. Baum's experience in business and life was deep. He shared it freely with Rich, and Rich listened well.

As with his coaches, Rich came to think of Baum as another natural mentor: "He took an active interest in me at a critical point in my life, helped me start building a vision for my future, gave me sound advice to help identify realistic goals, and had an especially positive impact on my life."

All that perspective came later, though. Right then Rich stayed focused on his next step: "After finishing the construction jobs in New Jersey in late spring of 1962, I enrolled in summer classes at St. Joseph's University, on the western edge of Philadelphia, to begin making up for the semester I'd missed at Susquehanna. While I took those classes, Russell Baum was living at his summer house in Ventnor and let me stay in his mansion in Merion Station, a town that borders west Philadelphia, is part of the storied Main Line, and is not far from St. Joseph's."

Baum's Merion Station home seemed to Rich enormous and exquisite: "Paintings lined the walls, especially the paintings of his uncle, Walter Emerson Baum, who'd died in 1956. Walter Baum, an artist who lived in the Allentown area, was well-known, not only for his art work but also for teaching free art classes to children in the Allentown School District. Since those classes were free, there was no money to spend on renting space, so he used the basement of the Allentown Art Museum for a studio classroom. The classes were informally referred to by locals as the Baum School. Rudy S. Ackerman, PhD, a local university professor who had an interest in the project, continued the Baum School legacy and taught art lessons after Walter Baum's death."

Rich was impressed by the extensive collection Baum had of his uncle's paintings: "He'd purchased over a hundred of them when

Walter was alive to support him financially. Russell Baum gave some of his uncle's paintings away to friends and displayed a select number of them in his beautiful home."

All of this was another form of mentoring for Rich. Anyone who drives down streets lined with luxurious homes gets glimpses into a world of wealth, but waking up each morning in one of those homes let Rich feel what it was like to inhabit such a life. His mother had made sure they had flowers, that there was beauty in their lives, even when there was no extra money for ice cream; he'd found a way to get the same hoagie Frank Sinatra ate; he'd felt at home in his friend David Aiken's "amazing house" in Margate. Now Russell Baum had given him—in addition to work, personal interest, and advice—a felt sense of living in a large, beautiful house filled with original art. Rich's vision of what was possible for his life was expanding in many directions.

Right then, though, the most visible expansion was in the family. Carmen, Rich's oldest sibling, had married a year or so before and was expecting his first child. Fran, the next oldest, got married in June that summer, while Rich was in summer school. By November, Christopher Caruso had arrived, making Rich an uncle. The stage was being set for Rich to do some mentoring of his own, which of course he'd realize only much later.

By that fall of 1962, as Rich got ready to return to Susquehanna for his sophomore year, Fran thought she saw a change in him. He seemed more mature and seemed to be thinking more about long-term goals.

He also wanted more independence. For one thing, he didn't want to live in a dorm. Neither did John Pignatore and Dick Hirsch, both of whom had signed the students' letter of support for Rich the spring before. They and Roger Forgerson had all been on the football team, and the four agreed to rent an apartment above a shoe store together. None of them had furniture or enough money to buy any, but Coach Garrett stayed tuned in to what was going on with his players. Getting enough sleep was part of training too, so he had the roommates meet him at the gym. From its attic he handed down to them the beds and mattresses they'd need to get started. They'd figure out the rest.

His teammates already saw Rich's football skills as outstanding, and John Pignatore described him as the scholar of their small group—a scholar who drove a white, blue-top Plymouth convertible: "When he wasn't around, we'd use his car to go dump our garbage. He'd reluctantly agreed we could, but he *really* didn't like garbage in his car!"

The four teammates' off-campus apartment became home to an ever-changing cast of students over the next three years. John was a senior that fall, so he graduated the spring of Rich's sophomore year. The next fall, another football player moved in: a transfer student named Bill Muir. Then during their senior year, Rich and Bill found a fifties-style motel at the edge of Selinsgrove. "There were five or six bungalows along the roadside," Bill recalls. "They were cheap with a tiny kitchen. We brought in two free cots from the nurses' room and found an old clothes wardrobe and a small table. There was no room left for anything else."

As he did with so many friends, Rich stayed in touch with Bill for decades, but Bill was easier to keep track of than most because his successes and job changes showed up in the sports pages. As Rich summarized it, "Bill enjoyed a successful career in the National Football League, as offensive coordinator or offensive line coach for eight NFL franchises, including the Tampa Bay Buccaneers, Philadelphia Eagles, and Kansas City Chiefs. He coached in two AFC/NFC Championship games and made twelve playoff appearances. Most notably, he served as offensive coordinator for the Buccaneers and helped lead them to a Super Bowl victory."

During his sophomore and junior years at Susquehanna, Rich was a starter on the football team, and he took extra classes each semester to make up for what he'd missed during the spring spent working on the boardwalk.

The summer of 1963, before his junior year, his sister, Fran, gave birth to her first child, Gerald Holtz—who soon became "Jerry" to everyone.

Rich got to see his nephews on some school breaks, but on every trip back home to Margate, he made sure to stop by Russell Baum's home in Merion Station to visit. This relationship and its "natural mentoring" developed into a lifelong friendship: "Even when I was unaware of what mentoring was and didn't see that it was occurring, my mentors from childhood and young adulthood often became my friends. As I matured and grew, our relationships became balanced partnerships. Since my connection with Russell Baum was so strong, he continued to mentor me as a close friend throughout the remaining decades of his life."

Baum also remained one of Rich's employers for a while: he paid Rich to do his personal accounting. Of course, Rich had other jobs too: "When I had time during the school year, I'd spend a few hours a week working at a gas station near St. Joseph's University to make extra money. Sophomore and junior summers I worked as a delivery truck driver when home in Margate and made a little more money at the gas station I'd worked for in high school."

During another of those college summers, Rich had a paper stand with his younger brother. Joe looked after the stand until 11:00 p.m., when Rich got there from his job as a waiter and took over, staying until the early hours of the morning.

Back at Susquehanna for his senior year, Rich never did cross paths with Sally Feitig, one of the pretty freshman girls enrolled that fall.

That's just as well, since he had to stay focused on football. During his sophomore season as a guard, Rich had been described in a local newspaper: "Caruso, 5-11, 190 pounder, has been the mainstay of the Crusaders' interior line, and in Coach Jim Garrett's words, 'has more than filled the shoes of graduated Little All-America Ben Di-Francesco.'" By the time Bill Muir and Rich began their senior year as roommates and teammates, Coach Garrett had selected Rich to be cocaptain of the team, and Bill thought he knew why: "Rich was tenacious, paid attention to detail, never took shortcuts, and never complained. The other players noticed. Rich was a role model, and he made the team better."

Rich had worked hard and taken initiative nearly all his life, mostly on his own. He'd figured out a more independent living situation at Susquehanna to give himself the freedom and flexibility he seemed to need. He'd developed lasting one-on-one friendships. He'd worked for many bosses. He'd earned promotions. He'd charted his own course.

This, though, was a step or two further along in his developing skill set. Now he had to listen to the coaches *and* get along with his cocaptain *and* think in terms of the entire team: "I came to realize that the success of the team as a whole depended on the individual development, effort, and success of each player. I focused on helping the team work together toward our shared objective of winning games by helping each player succeed in his own individual role, encouraging him to achieve his personal best." Where was that balance between individual needs and group goals? Rich was learning it as he taught it, and he was learning to mentor others while being mentored.

"From 1960 to 1965, Coaches Jim Garrett and Bob Pitello's combined team record was 40-3-1. This was the best five-year record of all of Susquehanna's sports teams. I received All Conference and All State honors and was proud to be a part of the team for the last four of those five years. Head Coach Garrett and his top assistant, Coach Pittello, were wonderful role models, responsible for the success of the team both on and off the field. So were the other coaches—most of them personal friends of Coach Garrett and all of them great to work with. Coaches Garrett and Pittello, though, made time to personally mentor me as well as many other players on the team."

Years later, Rich reflected, "I strongly believe that the best education I had in life was on the football field interacting with coaches and teammates. It's where I learned the value of collaborating. Since then, working with peers toward a mutually agreeable goal has brought me tremendous satisfaction. Those naturally occurring mentoring experiences positively shaped all of my professional life."

In fact, Coach Pittello's influence seems to have been a major factor even in Rich's choice of a major. On that first visit to Susquehanna, when Rich had been impressed by Pittello's handsome suit and Cadillac but learned that he was a coach instead of a professor, there was much more to learn. Bob Pittello had been a student and football player at Susquehanna, but when he coached Rich, he was also a full-time accountant: "Since he was working in accounting and was clearly successful, he was a major reason I decided to pursue an accounting major and a career in business myself. He had no children of his own, and I believe he thought of me as a son. We remained close friends until he died in 2011."

Bob Pittello gave Rich the idea that accounting could be part of his path; Russell Baum paid Rich to do his personal accounting, giving him practical experience as well as income; and they were only part of the team of mentors Rich became more aware of as he grew.

The end of 1964 was the end of college football for Rich. He had one semester of classes to go, but what then?

Before going home for Christmas, Rich got word that he'd landed an internship in the New York office of Main Lafrentz & Co., certified public accountants. The day after Christmas, Carmen's second son and Rich's third nephew, Charles Caruso, was born.

On January 25, 1965, Rich's internship at Lafrentz began, paying $475 a month. Seven weeks later, he'd been offered a full-time job for $575 a month, to begin when he graduated. Four years earlier, that would have seemed a big win to Rich, but he'd listened to his mentors' advice about this field he was entering: he'd go farther in accounting with a master's degree: "During the spring semester of 1965, my senior year at Susquehanna, I got concerned about what I'd do after graduating. I decided to see if I could go to graduate school, but the deadline for applying had passed in most schools. I wanted to visit any school before applying to it, so options were limited. Then I found Bucknell University, an excellent school only half an hour away from Susquehanna. I met with a professor there who knew me from my football career at Susquehanna, and we discussed the possibility of my attending graduate school at Bucknell. He said that if I were willing to do work for him and help teach classes, he'd be able to help me get an academic scholarship. I agreed and was accepted to pursue a graduate degree in economics: master of science in business administration (MSBA)."

The scholarship covered Rich's tuition in full, but not housing or other living expenses. Rich, of course, found a way: "I came across a small trailer for rent that was close to campus and inexpensive because it was near a state prison. I rented it for a year. In addition, I joined the Army Reserve, knowing that being called to duty for the Vietnam War was a possibility."

The summer of 1966, Rich graduated from Bucknell with a MSBA, and his sister, Fran, had her second child, David.

CHAPTER 3

SUPPORTING THE OLD WHILE STARTING THE NEW

1966 TO 1977

How could I be making money doing something that made me so happy?
—RICHARD E. CARUSO

With his days-old degree from Bucknell, Rich began work at Price Waterhouse in Philadelphia as an auditor. His first assignment was with its chief client, DuPont, in Wilmington, Delaware.

He'd enjoyed accounting in college, but auditing a large company became pretty routine pretty soon: "One day I came up with the idea to start a coin-flipping game among the accountants to see who'd pay for coffee when the cart arrived at ten o'clock. I looked forward to that game every day." It seemed to be the main thing at work Rich relished.

Was that it, then—the way he'd adapt to the reality of working in an office as a professional? He'd worked hard, for long hours, since grammar school. It had always been work toward his own goals, though, using his own strategies and always trying new things, always learning. He'd reached a kind of pinnacle: a professional with a graduate degree, no less; a good, regular paycheck. Would keeping the books straight for someone else's company be enough for Rich as long as he kept coming up with games to look forward to each morning?

His assignment to DuPont gave Rich some of the work experience required to earn his CPA. That period also gave him time to test his skills in an existing business, to build his confidence, *and* to realize that working for a Fortune 500 company didn't satisfy his entrepreneurial spirit: "In high school, I'd enjoyed fixing broken junk cars much more than just doing routine maintenance on cars in good condition. Since then, I'd come to feel strongly that helping financially struggling persons and companies was important—it meant something."

Within months, he'd made a plan and found the words: "I thanked Price Waterhouse for assigning me to such a respected client and then asked to be assigned instead to start-ups, developing companies struggling to find success." In 1967, around the end of Rich's first year with Price, they'd assigned him to an audit with a new company in Pennsylvania called Lease Financing Corporation.

Later, Rich wrote of that time: "With experience in accounting, legal, lending, and other sectors, five talented employees were working together in a small office to establish LFC as a big-ticket equipment-leasing company. Leasing was a smart option for companies with limited financial means needing specialized equipment to run their businesses on a day-to-day basis. Leasing required less cash up front than buying did, and it let a company devote more capital to other aspects of its business and grow revenue faster. Leasing also allowed companies to acquire the newest technologies at reasonable pricing levels. By the time I began working with it, LFC had already started leasing equipment to businesses, and it had used an intelligent strategy: keeping each lease in a separate LFC-managed company so that one failed endeavor wouldn't negatively impact other leases."

It felt like a good fit for Rich, and Price Waterhouse kept him assigned there for about two years, as Rich went right on developing his life.

For one thing, he was still completing his commitment to the Army Reserve: as a sergeant in medical detachment, repairing medical equipment. That may have seemed a random placement at the time, but one year in college Rich had joined the Biemic Society, designed to "keep its members informed on current scientific events." He also knew how to repair cars and buildings—did the military think that might mean he'd be good at fixing other things too? Most interesting, though, was that his experience with medical devices later turned out to be one of the bridges to a significant part of Rich's life, almost as if it were planned.

At around this same time, Rich got to know Henry Haines, who was in the reserve too. They found a two-bedroom apartment in Wynnewood to rent together. One bedroom was bigger than the other; and, as Henry remembered it, "Rich, ever the negotiator, told me, 'I'll pay five dollars more a month for the bigger bedroom.'" Those extra square feet came in handy later.

Henry and Rich went to reserve meetings and summer camps together too, traveling to Colorado, Texas, and other states. As they stood in formation at one reserve meeting in Georgia, Henry noticed that Rich's shoes weren't polished and looked as if they had chocolate on them: "I told Rich to rub his shoes in the wet grass, and he did. When the inspector got to us, Rich's shoes still looked shiny from the wetness, and the inspector complimented him on a good shoeshine job. Rich was lucky that way."

Henry learned that Rich had an active mind, got very excited when learning new things, and was curious about almost everything. Once, soon after the first cell phones had come out and they were in a car together, Rich used his new cell to call an associate in England, just because he could.

Henry also got used to Rich having a lot on his mind: "One day I came back to the apartment and found egg bits everywhere: ceiling, walls, floor. Rich had put on a dozen eggs to boil and then left the apartment, and the eggs had exploded all over the kitchen. I cleaned up the mess but didn't mention it until about four months later, when Rich said, 'Oh, no, I forgot all about them!'"

The years of playing football were over for Rich, but he'd learned to ski and occasionally went on ski trips. Henry did too and remembered how generous Rich was: "Sometimes if I didn't have the money to go skiing with him, he'd say, 'Come on, I'll pay. Let's go.' He didn't expect anything in return. He was always trying to think how he could make a contribution to the world, wanted to do good for people. He was tough in other ways, liked to win with his business plans, but he had that softer side—and a strong sense of family."

Fran would vouch for that. She may have known Rich's softer side better than anyone. While he was navigating this new life he'd created, she was navigating marriage. In 1967, when Rich had been assigned to LFC, Fran had decided that she needed to go back to work. She and her husband lived in an apartment in Bellmawr, New Jersey, with their two young sons, and her husband's struggles with gambling and alcohol addiction were getting in the way of supporting his family. Research on healing addiction was still sparse and hadn't been translated into programs that helped. Most people still thought of addiction as a moral weakness rather than an illness. Fran didn't have any of the resources or support she might have accessed a few decades later; but she did have family, and she knew how to work.

They moved back to her parents' home in Margate so her mother could take care of Jerry and David while Fran went back to the secretarial job she'd had when she was single and while she kept on trying to keep her marriage and family together.

In August 1967, Carmen's third child was born: a girl this time, named Bonnie. She was Louise and Cono's fifth grandchild, Richard's first niece, and Fran was expecting again.

In 1968, her daughter, Dana, was born, and Fran soon felt that, with three children, she needed to move out of her parents' home. Rich had been trying to help before, but he hadn't known how to heal anyone's addictions either. He did know what to do now, though. He helped her, emotionally and financially, to buy her own home, not far from their parents in Margate.

Later, when divorce proceedings began, Fran's hurt, angry husband left, taking their only car. She had no way to get to work, and she remembered clearly what happened next: "Rich drove over from Pennsylvania and insisted on leaving his used Lincoln Continental with me, saying it was no trouble for him to take the train to work. A few months later, he showed up with a used Volkswagen Beetle for me to keep." She also remembered that "it was always breaking down. It had a motor in the back, and Rich put bricks under the hood to give the front more weight—to make it safer, he said."

After that, Rich showed up frequently. Fran remembered that "even when Rich had his first job after college and made very little money, he'd help me out all the time. He'd come to see us and try to give me money. I'd say, 'No, no, no!' I didn't want to take his money, but about fifteen minutes after leaving, he'd call and say he'd seen a twenty-dollar bill in the bookcase. He'd hide money for me to find so I'd have to keep it."

He began bringing toys and games for her children at Christmas, and he checked in on day-to-day practical things too. When a floor covering wore out, Fran replaced it with linoleum that she soon realized was faulty. She mentioned it to Rich, who wrote to the manufacturer and met a service rep at Fran's house. The man said the problem was in the subfloor, so he wouldn't be able to replace the linoleum. Rich said, "Well then, I guess we'll just rip it out and see if it's the subfloor." The rep agreed to replace the linoleum.

Fran's memories of that time stayed fresh for the rest of her life: "I don't know what I'd have done without Rich helping me out, but I never had to ask him for help. It's what was in his heart."

Meanwhile, Rich had completed his commitment to the Army Reserve without being deployed overseas, and LFC was expanding. The economy was thriving, and the company saw an increase in leasing activity. Due to this growth, LFC needed to hire more employees and asked Rich if he'd like to join their company: "I was excited and interested in being involved with the development of a start-up; so in 1969, after about three years with Price Waterhouse, I accepted LFC's offer and resigned from my auditing position at Price."

By then, Rich had met the experience requirement to earn his CPA, had passed all parts of the exam in a single sitting, and had become certified as a public accountant.

Not too many months later, Rich had a fifth nephew. In March 1970, Carmen's fourth child, John Caruso, was born. That meant Louise and Cono had seven grandchildren—but none yet from Rich.

Just as Rich joined LFC, its president, an attorney, announced that he was retiring and had selected another lawyer, Frank Slattery, to be the new president: "Frank and I started at the same time and served together at LFC for over twenty years. We both held positions on the board of directors. Eventually, I assumed the role of executive vice president and worked with Frank to build LFC into a large, successful company." That growth began fast: "Soon after starting to work together, Frank and I met with Fred Smith, who wanted to lease aircraft and start an overnight delivery service to compete with the US Postal Service. That entity, to become FedEx, was in its initial planning stages when we took on the project. I connected with several businesses and banks, finding used aircraft for his company. With a later prospective client, Ted Turner's Cable News Network (CNN), we experienced the same rapid success as with FedEx. With our advice and support, CNN developed into the first national television network of its kind."

The pace suited Rich: "It felt good to see how quickly the start-ups we worked with became self-sufficient and prosperous. The free-flowing collaboration with them, applying our skills to their ideas and coming up with creative solutions, brought some phenomenal results."

Having great success within their own company in only a short period of time was definitely gratifying, but something else was going on within Rich too: "We felt we were making a positive difference for the entire country. By helping small, innovative businesses get established, we were also stimulating the economy." He was contributing, and that's what mattered to Rich: giving as well as getting.

Yet there seemed to be an even deeper level to how Rich thought about life. He experienced what he called "great personal satisfaction," but it came from more than finally having enough extra money for ski trips and helping his sister. It was more than expanding markets, or contributing to the economy, or even the deep human connections that come with teamwork. He saw his work as part of helping other people's dreams come true, and he felt enriched by their success as well as his own. Helping them filled a need in him.

All that enrichment kept growing for Rich, and LFC kept growing too: "After seeing such growth for FedEx and CNN, another start-up, Microwave Communications Incorporated (MCI), asked us to help them create and implement low-cost, long-distance tele-phone calls. We decided to fund this venture, which later became Verizon."

Rich continued thinking of strategies to help new clients: "One of them was Philadelphia Electric Company (PECO). It wanted to join with other power and light companies to form a pool that reduced electric costs for all members. LFC helped that happen by providing financing for the computer equipment needed by these companies, later called the Pennsylvania-New Jersey-Maryland Interconnection. This PJM Interconnection, LLC, headquartered in Valley Forge, made it possible for companies with excess energy to sell that excess to members who needed more to meet the needs of their customers. Ultimately, PJM became part of the Eastern Interconnection grid, coordinating the movement of electricity throughout all or parts of Pennsylvania, New Jersey, Maryland, and ten other states plus the District of Columbia. More than one thousand companies became members of PJM, which came to serve more than six million customers, saving them millions of dollars."

As part of that now huge regional grid, PECO still had the job of managing its local circuits, so it turned to LFC again. This time, PECO needed to increase its ability to keep power flowing consistently from substations to its growing customer base. To do so, LFC helped it become part of the national energy producer Exelon Corporation.

As times changed, LFC's client base kept growing, mainly through word of mouth: "One of our biggest customers was International Business Machines (IBM) after a federal legal deci-sion required it to sell rather than lease its equipment. Many had leased because they hadn't had the funds to buy, so IBM's revenue dropped with this ruling. LFC capitalized on the change by using its company funds to buy equipment from IBM and then lease it to clients at a much lower cost than IBM charged. We later supported other computer-equipment companies in the same way, buying their supply at a low cost, which gave them funds to manufacture and sell additional equipment."

Rich and Frank often helped LFC do well by doing good: "As US highways were being publicly funded in the 1950s and 1960s, more and more people could travel using their own cars. By the 1960s and 70s, many railroad companies were failing, including Pennsylvania Railroad. It had been bought in 1968 by New York Central Railroad, another financially unstable company. The two merged and by 1969 were named Penn Central Transportation Company. Frank and I, starting together at LFC then, knew Penn Central could easily go bankrupt. It soon did, but we wanted to support it anyway because so many people in our area relied on it for travel. We helped it lease high-speed Metroliner trains to go between Washington, DC, New York, and Boston. United Aircraft's Turbo Train operated a Boston-to-New York line, and on January 16, 1971, these rail services merged into Amtrak, the US government's national passenger train service."

Rich, Frank, and LFC had kept Penn Central alive long enough to assure that passenger service between Philly, Boston, New York, and DC would survive.

"With another railroad project, we leased freight trains to independent companies that moved coal from Pennsylvania mines to cargo ships headed for China. Other times, we restored companies in order to keep their jobs in the area. Often we got involved in restructuring corporations so they could keep doing business with their same employees, in the same community."

It was a busy time for Rich. He had financial success, got to pull together resources on a much larger scale than when he'd commandeered his father's shoe-shining equipment, and got to help others in the process.

He and Henry also fit in some ski trips. On one of them, Rich noticed a vivacious blonde woman and felt attracted to the warmth in her laugh. Friends from Susquehanna introduced him to her. He learned that she taught 3rd grade in Allentown and had graduated from Susquehanna three years after he had. Her name was Sally—she was that pretty freshman he hadn't met during his busy senior year.

Back at home, Rich called and asked her to go out with him on New Year's Eve. As they saw each other more, her big curiosity about life seemed to match his. A year and a half later, when Rich asked her to marry him, Sally said yes but explained that there was an additional step to the process. He had to ask her father for her hand in marriage. Maybe Rich saw it as just an old-school tradition, but it wasn't completely perfunctory. Mr. Feitig did agree to the proposal, but he said no to another request. Rich asked Sally to go on a vacation to Europe before they were married, but her father said no to that one: "No vacations together before marriage!"

On August 5, 1972, Sally Feitig and Rich Caruso were married in the Poconos at the prerevolutionary home that had been in Sally's family for six generations. There was a walk-in fireplace in the kitchen, and the house was filled with memories of all the good times Sally and her friends had had there. A creek ran through the property, on which there were also an old church, a school house, and a beautiful garden with an arbor. That's where the ceremony took place: exactly where Sally had always wanted to have her wedding.

They went on a wedding trip to Jamaica. When they got home, Rich went back to live with Henry, and Sally lived in an apartment in Bethlehem for six months, working at a job there to complete requirements for her teacher certification. Then she moved into the two-bedroom apartment in Wynnewood that Rich still shared

with Henry. That extra five dollars a month Rich had been paying to have the larger bedroom seemed an especially good deal
right then.

Henry quipped that Sally stole Rich away from him when,
before long, they bought and moved to a house in King of Prussia,
Pennsylvania. That's where they lived when Jonathan was born in
December 1974 and Peter in June 1977. Sally had grown up in a
Protestant family, Rich in a Catholic one, and it felt important to
him that his boys be raised in the faith he knew. Sally agreed
to raise them as Catholics and, when the time came, took them
both to the church's CCD classes for children. She even learned
from her mother-in-law how to cook Italian meals for all of them.

Becoming a parent does change everything, but Rich had a
head start on this stage in life—he'd been practicing. He'd kept
on showing up at Fran's house in Margate, doing his best to be a
father figure for her three children.

Fran's youngest, Dana, described the routine she and David
and Jerry had with Uncle Rich: "When he came to our house as
we were growing up, he'd sit in a chair in Mom's living room and
talk to each of us individually. First, Jerry would go in as Uncle
Rich sat in his chair. Then David would go in. Then I would go
in. He wanted to take stock of how we were doing. At that time, I
sort of dreaded the questions and conversation because I felt I was
being assessed. Back then, he seemed to me a distant father figure,
seemed closer to Jerry and David."

Over time, Dana realized how big a safety net Uncle Rich provided for all of them. She noticed that he was always there when
needed. She also learned that he believed in them, believed that
all of them could figure out their own solutions and "do for ourselves." He'd help, but he'd also ask, "What are you going to do?"

David remembered looking up to his Uncle Rich, wanting to be
like him, and not ever wanting to disappoint him. He remembered

Rich telling him to "learn as much as you can," "find different ways to see," "get out of your comfort zone," and, always, "chart your own course."

David also called his uncle "a role model for working hard," remembering Rich loading his pickup truck with tools, climbing ladders to repair roofs of buildings he'd bought, and for at least one of his buildings, being on the construction site ten to twelve hours a day checking the quality of the work even though he had a project manager. It was David too who watched *how* Rich did physical labor alongside the other workers: "He had great empathy for others."

Jerry was the oldest, five or six, when Uncle Rich began filling in some of the cracks in his life. He remembers Rich as "The Enforcer," sometimes talking to Jerry on the phone and asking, "Do I need to come over there to see about things?" when, as Jerry put it later, "I needed to be told to behave." As he got older and into sports, Jerry remembered with a wry grin that Uncle Rich "never got after me for my grades, but he'd bring protein drinks that tasted terrible and healthy chips or other food he thought would be good for me."

Rich's parents got to see their son help his sister in ways they couldn't. Cono had felt helpless anger when Fran's husband had been unable to provide even the basics for her. Louise had felt her daughter's hurt and had dealt with that hurt by taking care of Fran's children while Fran worked long hours. It was Rich, though, who'd given Fran the help she needed to provide a home for her children. Louise had felt deep relief in seeing Rich step in. It was October 1978, when Peter was nearly seventeen months old, that Louise passed away. By then she'd seen that Rich's own family was well started, and she knew that Rich would fill in the gaps well enough for Fran and her children to be all right.

Before his mother died, Rich had met with Jerry, thirteen, and David, ten (and would meet with Dana a few years later). Uncle Rich told them that he and Aunt Sally had set aside money for their college, so now it was up to them to get the good grades they'd need to get into college.

Rich remembered how he had almost dropped out of high school at fourteen, sure he couldn't go to college because his parents couldn't pay for it. He wanted to be sure Fran's children didn't make the mistake he almost had. He wanted them to know they could reach bigger goals.

Jerry felt surprised, knowing his family didn't have much money and assuming Uncle Rich didn't either. He sure didn't act rich! Once, when Jerry was going to babysit Jonathan and Peter, Uncle Rich said he'd take Jerry and the boys out to eat first. He picked Jerry up in an old station wagon that had a hole in the floorboard. They rolled the windows down so exhaust fumes from under the car would go right back out. At the restaurant, Rich paid for their meal with cash he took from a paper bag he'd brought with him. "Rich was never pretentious, and you never knew he was wealthy," Jerry said later.

Rich also told them that the set-aside money was for *only* college. Jerry, good at sports and at thirteen already becoming a negotiator like his uncle, asked if he could have the money if he got a college scholarship. Rich thought for a minute and said yes . . . which led to some interesting complications later.

The year after that college talk, Jerry was about to start high school in Atlantic City. Students from Margate would make up only 10 percent of the student body, so 90 percent of those in the new school wouldn't know his name: it seemed the perfect time to carry out a plan he had to change his last name to Caruso. Fran said to ask Uncle Rich what he thought. Uncle Rich said, "Jerry, the man makes the name; the name doesn't make the man." Jerry understood and kept his name.

The life lessons in marriage often come from differences in the couple's backgrounds, and Sally and Rich had as many differences as any other couple: ethnicity and religion, of course, but others too. Her family had had enough extra money for ice cream, and his hadn't; her family had lived in America for at least six generations, and his . . . barely for one; she hadn't had to fight, to be tough, to feel safe in high school, and he had. Of course there were other differences, but a core value they shared, and lived, was holding family close and helping others. Fran always felt that Sally's support for her and her children was just as strong as Rich's, that Sally chose not to resent her husband acting as a father to other children as well as their own, chose not to resent Rich spending time with Fran's family when he'd been at work long hours already and his wife and children needed him too. It couldn't have been easy for Sally at times, but that warmth Rich had noticed in her had been, apparently, quite deep. Her empathy for others seemed to fully match his. Whatever life lessons their marriage presented, differing on whether to help others seemed not to be one of them. "Sally was wonderful" was Fran's summary.

CHAPTER 4

GROWING A COMPANY; GROWING A FAMILY

1977 TO 1986

It's not the deal; it's the people you deal with.
—RICHARD CARUSO

A couple of years after Peter's birth, and months after Louise's death, Cono finally retired from his last job as a waiter. He was eighty-five. He'd worked for nearly seventy years and been married for more than forty. He'd gotten a little crotchety, a little "stubborn," as the family sometimes called him. Some of them came to understand that the stubbornness had helped him make it in this country he'd first seen as a teen, helped him pay for two houses on a waiter's income, helped him launch this very American family. He and Louise had lived in their Margate house for almost a quarter of a century by then. They'd gone through a lot together, ups and downs. The place felt sort of empty without her . . . full of memories, though. The grandchildren remembered the house, their grandmother's sewing machine with foot pedals, big family dinners (often on Sundays after church and especially on Thanksgiving), great Italian food (well, for Jerry, it was his grandmother's "terrific hamburgers"), Cono and Sally having heated discussions, the grandchildren playing after meals while their fathers and uncles "looked like they were in a coma from eating so much, sitting in front of the TV watching a football game." Cono stayed there for the rest of his life.

Rich and Sally took him out to dinner occasionally, once to the Seaview Country Club, the place he'd taken three buses to get to when he'd waited tables there. "I'm on the other side now," Cono said that night.

They also finally talked him into going on a trip to his hometown in Sicily. Jonathan and Peter were still little, so they stayed with Sally's parents, but Cono's brother, "Uncle Joe," went along. Rich relished giving his father this gift.

With double family responsibilities by then, Rich, just as his father had, kept right on working. Growing LFC, he and Frank Slattery found that many of their customers wanted to lease real estate in addition to the equipment LFC already offered. When LFC's board voted *not* to lease real estate, Rich felt the company would lose customers and asked to handle it as a personal project.

The board approved his request, so in 1978, the year after Peter was born, Rich provided real-estate leasing for LFC's clients by creating the first of a series of limited partnerships, which laid the groundwork for what would become the Provco Group Ltd. Over the years, through Provco, Rich acquired more than fifty properties that required very little time and attention once the lease was in place. It was an impressive portfolio of commercial real estate, and he amassed it with very little help from others.

During that period, accountant Gary DiLella came to LFC and began getting to know Rich. Soon, with the LFC board's approval, Rich hired Gary to work nights and weekends on the accounting and taxes related to this real estate venture. All of this was not so much a "business," Rich would say, as an "opportunity" that complemented the work he was still doing with LFC.

Around then, the majority of LFC's shares were bought by a Philadelphia bank, Provident National Corporation (PNC), a public company. The requisite financial reports for PNC and LFC showed that LFC was more financially successful than the bank. Eventually, PNC sold its LFC shares to a private diversified holding company, Cawsl Corporation, based in the Philadelphia area. Rich and his partners were required to sell their LFC shares to Cawsl also but were allowed a period of time before doing so. Rich waited as long as possible to sell, pretty sure that the business would grow during that time, so the value of his shares would increase. He was handsomely rewarded for his patience.

Over the next two decades Gary saw Rich make and lose money, take bad deals and fix them, analyze risk and find ways to minimize it, sometimes be the one voice of reason in a room when he felt there was too much risk, and often get hold of a deal he believed in and not let go—like a pit bull. They learned from each other and became friends. In 2000 Gary would become the CFO of Provco. By then, he and Rich had worked together on more deals than either took time to count.

Rich was one of the first of a breed referred to today as serial entrepreneurs. His intellect and vision saw what others couldn't. He had what Gary heard someone call a "3-D–chess mind." He'd see several moves ahead when contemplating a transaction and think about its effects from different angles and time frames.

He also found time to pursue other interesting and challenging business opportunities, which was just a way of playing for Rich—like moving pieces around on a big game board.

One example is the first large entrepreneurial deal he structured: buying and selling Rustler Steak Houses.

It began one day in 1981 when Rich met Jim Sullivan at lunch in Villanova. Jim worked for Marriott Corporation at that time, and

Marriott had decided to grow its fast-food restaurant business, the Roy Rogers roast beef chain. To do so, they bought the Gino's hamburger chain but were saddled with the money-losing Rustler chain in the deal. Jim was assigned to turn this scenario around. His plan was to convert the most profitable Gino's locations to Roy Rogers restaurants, sell the remaining Gino's, and sell the entire Rustler chain. This had to happen fast. Remember, they're losing money!

To get started, Jim went to Gino's headquarters, located in King of Prussia. Rich lived there then, *and* he'd done some Gino's leases, so he knew its controller, Don Tomasso, who set up that lunch. Don wondered if Rich might want to buy Rustler.

Rich might, and talks with Jim Sullivan began . . . until a funny thing happened. As Jim remembered it, "about halfway through the negotiations, Richard said that he liked me and wanted me to join him as president of Rustler. I immediately called Richard Marriott and decided to join Rich" on the condition that Jim didn't have to move from Maryland, where he and his family lived. Also, Jim didn't have any money to invest, so he negotiated with Rich a way to buy into the Rustler deal over time.

More than thirty years later, Jim clearly remembered what came next: "Marriott still wanted me to finish negotiating the sale. That put me in a strange ethical dilemma, but it all ended well with Rich creating Tenly Enterprises, through which he and other investors bought Rustler. The deal required using a lot of bank debt. Since Rustler had a negative cash flow, the bank required both Rich and me to guarantee the debt, which we did. I immediately began focusing on turning Rustler to a positive cash flow, which we did in our first year and each year thereafter. Rich would call me every night to find out what was going on in the business."

Both Jim and Rich's brother Carmen bought shares in Rustler, but those shares were also made available to Herb Brown and others working for LFC.

Herb had worked for LFC about eight years by then, drawing up documents for deals Rich negotiated—and, of course, becoming friends: "My wife Barbara and I were going on a ten-day Caribbean cruise on a ship called *The Sea Goddess*, and I asked Rich if he and Sally would like to go with us. On the first night, Barbara and Sally came down to dinner with the same dress on!" After they'd all laughed about it, Sally slipped out and changed to something else. The four took another cruise together as well, to St. Thomas, and the friendship between Rich and Herb soon included their wives. Sally put it simply: "Barbara and I were friends and had fun together."

Herb called working with Rich "fun" too because "I could never tell what he'd say or do. Once, Wall Street lawyers wanted a contract on a large ship-leasing deal to include liability to LFC. They broke to discuss, came back together, and Rich summarized: 'We'll be responsible but not liable!' They took the deal."

Herb chuckled when remembering: "Another time, Rich brought his young son Jonathan and me to an important meeting with a dozen high-powered lawyers. Jonathan wandered around outside the meeting for a while and then came into the conference room and gave a lollipop to everyone there." Later Herb grinned at that image of lawyers sitting around in three-piece suits sucking on lollipops.

When Herb introduced Rich to computers at LFC, they got into a conversation about numbers and soon got in a contest: "I'd enter numbers into the computer to get totals, but it turned out Rich could calculate the sums in his head faster than I could enter them! Other times, in discussing deals, Rich could calculate in his mind any changes the other side wanted, figuring out on the spot whether the change would make money for LFC. He could answer right away and saved us many extra meetings. He also understood very complicated deals. Often the other party thought Rich was a lawyer because he spoke like one and understood all the legal details."

Herb was also impressed that Rich never had a personal secretary. He just had various secretaries type things for him. "Rich didn't believe in frills" was how Herb saw it.

When Rich bought Rustler, though, Herb was impressed at an even deeper level: "He told every investor that he, Rich, would be getting an override of 10 percent of the profits, letting us all know up front that he'd get more than anyone else. He worked on it night and day. He was on the phone all the time. He saw it through, and we all felt he deserved that 10 percent. The difference in working with Rich was that he'd tell everyone the details of the deal up front. He was honest and transparent. Others would work on deals and not tell anyone they were taking extra money, but you'd find out later. We all knew what Rich was doing and never resented his making extra money."

Over the years, many other people saw that "difference in working with Rich." He became increasingly adept at restructuring failing businesses and transforming them into cash cows in a way that benefitted all concerned, not just himself. Once he bought foreclosed railcars, negotiated a deal that gave the lender 100 percent of its principal, and allowed the fleet to keep operating in a way that generated revenue for years to come.

Another time, he bought a failing coal fired plant, turned it around, and sold it for a big profit to the utility plant operating it. Many companies do such restructuring, but the way Rich did it left those involved feeling it was fair. He'd get the help he needed and compensate those helping him with not only salary and fees but also a share of the profit if the venture succeeded. In Rich's way of doing business, the interests of all the stakeholders were aligned. It was smart business. It was the right thing to do. It was at the core of who Rich was.

Early in his life Rich had determined *never* to be bullied again. Many people stop there, thinking their only choices are bully or be bullied, win or lose, power-over or power-under. He came to see those choices as a made-up game, not the reality he wanted. What did the old "Do-unto-others" idea look like in business? Maybe he could figure that out. Around then the catch-word for such thinking was "win-win." Later "power-with" showed up. His grandchildren might call it just "sustainable." Whatever it was called, it's what made sense to him, so that's what he'd keep trying to do.

It was in 1979, the same year his father retired and before most of his playing-for-the-good-of-all-concerned businesses got going, when Rich learned that his friend and mentor Russell Baum had died at ninety-six. Rich was in his thirties, and he could feel his world shifting.

One way he'd adapt to this change was to put reminders of Russell around him. He and Sally went to Baum's estate and bought art: "Many beautiful things," Sally recalled, "but without a place to put them. I kept thinking we were buying too many; where would they go?" There was definitely not room at their house in King of Prussia, so the art they'd bought would have to be stored. Many pieces went to Sally's parents' home while Rich and Sally looked for a bigger house—someplace that would be perfect for all of it.

Meanwhile, Rich learned that Baum, with all his business savvy, hadn't made a clear plan for how his wealth was to be used after he was gone. He had made provision for his sister, though, which involved Rich: "Before Russell's death, I promised him that I'd take care of his sister, who was very ill. He put money in his will for me to do so, saying that I was to keep any money left after she passed away. The best care I could find for her was in a nursing home, and she lived there for two years before her own death."

Then Rich had to decide what to do with the funds remaining. He felt a special connection to the Baum School of Art because of his long relationship with Russell of course, but there was an Italian tie too: a twenty-four-foot statue, *Leonardo's Horse*, sculpted following the detailed instructions and illustrations made by da Vinci for the duke of Milan in 1482. The first rendering of da Vinci's design had been given to Italy by the US years earlier, and a reproduction of it by Nina Akamu was at the Baum School. What to do seemed obvious to Rich. To others his decision seemed creative, generous, and savvy—Rich at his best.

He chose two ways to honor his dear friend: "First, I made a contribution to the Baum School of Art, then run by Dr. Rudy S. Ackerman out of the basement of the Allentown Art Museum. The gift let Dr. Ackerman create the new Baum School of Art in its own building. Second, I purchased about fifty of Walter Baum's paintings from Russell Baum's collection and donated them to the school. Long-term leasing of these paintings to businesses and other organizations generated a steady source of revenue for the school and so sustained its nonprofit mission of enriching lives through art." Rich had given the school a home as well as a way to carry out its work sustainably—a way for Russell's gift of mentoring to keep on giving for generations.

Money remained in Baum's estate after both of those gifts, and Rich wanted to use it in some way that would make an especially positive impact. He thought about how to do that while he kept on working and trying to fill in as father for Fran's children.

During his senior year in high school, Jerry was dating a girl at Boston College and felt it crucial to have his own car for their dates. The one he wanted cost $2,300, and he had only $300. Uncle Rich insisted he work for things he wanted. *Hmmm . . .* what to do? Jerry thought he'd gotten a great deal when Uncle Rich gave him $1,500 and Uncle Joe gave him $500, so his own $300 was enough . . . until he took an expensive first trip to Boston in his own car. When Jerry got home, the phone rang: it was Uncle Rich asking how the trip went. And by the way, had he happened to get any speeding tickets? Jerry had gotten three—and Rich let him solve that problem by himself.

Rich had attended Jerry's baseball games whenever he could during much of the past decade. In the spring of 1981, Jerry was about to graduate from high school and had several offers to consider: scholarships from Cornell, Miami, and Villanova, *or* to be drafted by the Philadelphia Phillies! The rule was that only parents could sign contracts for high school students, but Uncle Rich went to sign for Jerry when he met with the Phillies. When he was told he couldn't represent his nephew, Rich said, "Well, that makes him a free agent."

That strategy might not have worked for everyone, but Rich felt sure the Phillies didn't want to lose Jerry. Scouts were saying, "Jerry Holtz has the best infield arm seen this year. He is a 'find' from Atlantic City High School, runs a 6.6-second sixty, and has a rifle arm at shortstop."[*]

The Phillies offered him $50,000. It seemed a huge amount to Jerry. "Not really a lot for a lifetime," Uncle Rich thought, so they talked about the importance of education. Jerry took the Cornell scholarship.

Almost as soon as he got on campus, though, he learned that Cornell had dropped fall baseball, and other things weren't what he'd expected either. Jerry called Uncle Rich and said, "Get me out of here. Get me out of here." Was the Villanova scholarship offer still good? Rich called the coach, found out it was, and told Jerry to drive down right away so he'd get there in time for baseball

---

[*] Kerrane, Kevin. *Dollar Sign on the Muscle: The World of Baseball Scouting* (Lexington, KY: Prospectus Entertainment Ventures, 2013), 149.

practice. Jerry didn't have his car and wasn't old enough to rent one on his own, so Rich arranged to rent a car for him. Jerry made it to practice. He also took note of the schooling he'd just gotten from his uncle: (a) Focus on the goal. (b) If one strategy doesn't work, try another.

On the first day of practice, Villanova's coach went over Jerry's scholarship with him. It didn't cover all expenses, and Jerry owed some money he didn't have. Uncle Rich promised to figure it out and told Jerry not to worry. Rich could have easily paid the extra money, but something about it must have seemed unfair to him because a bit of his teenage tough-guy persona came out. The next day at practice, the coach called Jerry over and said, "It's OK, you don't owe any money—but tell your uncle not to threaten me again!"

Jerry got his scholarship and earned it by setting a school career record for home runs. Uncle Rich gave him the money set aside for college, and Jerry became lifelong friends with the Villanova coach, who later coached Jerry's son Nicholas in high school.

During the same year that Jerry was settling into college, 1981, Rich and Sally found their big house. It was an old mansion on a hill off Conestoga Road in Villanova, and they began an extensive renovation. Rich, of course, was right in the middle of it all. He did much of the work himself, every weekend, often until ten or eleven at night.

It took months, but after the four Carusos moved into their spacious new home, there was plenty of room for company. They were now in Villanova, not far from the university, and Jerry wound up living with them for a couple of years. Later Fran's two younger children stayed there too: David for about a year, and Dana for several months. As Carmen's daughter, Bonnie, grew up, she'd sometimes come over to babysit Jonathan and Peter. Sally put on two big Christmas dinners each year, one for her family and one for Rich's—in addition to the many other parties and dinners that she and Rich hosted over the years. Their home was both art-filled and welcoming. They used it well.

Still, they left it sitting empty for a month most summers, when Rich rented a beach house in Ocean City, New Jersey, joining Sally and the boys on weekends. Sally's parents usually came down for a week or two also, which Jon and Peter relished. Time at the beach hadn't been a part of Rich's childhood. To give that experience to his children had special meaning for him.

It was actually in 1980, the year before he and Sally found their big house, that Rich had gotten into the horse business. He became a partner in a corporation formed to breed thoroughbred horses on a farm in Chester Springs, Pennsylvania. Broodmares were shipped to be bred with stallions in various places. After breeding, the mares returned to Chester Springs to have their foals born and raised there. Initially, there were five horses on the farm. Within a few years there were sixty.

There were seven partners in the corporation. Most were interested primarily in the tax advantages of owning horses, but Rich was interested in the horses themselves. He found horse racing fascinating and learned that others did too. People who asked him what business he was in generally liked hearing about horse racing more than any of his other ventures.

One thing Rich liked about the horse business was Jeff Robbins, who was talented in training horses and telling stories. He liked to tell one about Prince Charles coming to a horse sale and asking to see some yearlings owned by Rich and the partnership. Jeff and Prince Charles stood side by side, each sipping a Bloody Mary, while the prince's bodyguard stood discreetly to the side, never taking his eyes off Jeff.

Jeff lived on the Chester Springs farm with his wife, Pat, and their twin girls, who were a few months younger than Jonathan. Rich, Sally, and the boys would go to the farm to see horses or attend the annual picnic, and the two families became friends. It was one place where Rich's work life and family life met.

Sally said that Rich never talked to her about business or his life at work and never seemed upset about anything there. It was almost as if he had two separate lives, she thought, but there was at least one other way he bridged work and home. Rich tried to be more involved in his sons' lives than his father had been in his, and occasionally Rich would take Jon and Peter to his office.

As an adult, Peter still remembered, "My dad used to take us to work with him at LFC when we were quite young. Jon and I worked in the copy room weighing mail and putting on postage. After we worked, we'd go to his office and visit with Dad. Later, we learned the concept of interest and how money grew in value when kept in an account."

Along with all the other parts of his life, Rich had, by the fall of 1982, overseen completion of another improvement to their new home: laying cobblestones in front of the house to create a huge cul-de-sac. It was finished by the time Jonathan was in 2nd grade and Peter in kindergarten. That's when Rich decided to write a letter to John Crosby, superintendent of the Radnor Township School District.

Decades later, Dr. Crosby remembered that letter clearly: "As usual, Rachel Dale, my secretary, had placed the morning mail on my desk. On top of the stack was a typewritten letter from Mr. Richard E. Caruso, on LFC stationery, stating that he believed his two young sons were being picked up at a hazardous bus stop on Conestoga Road. He requested that the bus, instead, stop in front of his house, up a winding driveway two hundred yards from the designated pickup point. Mr. Caruso felt that as the big yellow bus came over the hill and stopped at the bottom of his driveway, a vehicle following behind it could ram the rear of the bus and injure his sons as they were getting on.

"I picked up the phone and reached Mr. Caruso. Picturing that stretch of road, I told him that Jake McCarthy, director of transportation, tried to make all bus stops safe. I explained that the Pennsylvania school code required bus stops to be nonhazardous, although assessment of safety was subjective.

"Mr. Caruso suggested that the bus driver could drive up the driveway and pick up the boys in the cul-de-sac in front of his house. I explained that school board policy prohibited buses from turning around in cul-de-sacs because backing up while children were getting on and off is dangerous. Caruso countered that when he moved to his renovated home, he'd constructed a cul-de-sac large enough for a fire truck to circle without having to back up. I said that, regardless, there'd be no exceptions, but I'd be glad to meet him at the bus stop the next morning to observe the bus as it picked up Jonathan and Peter. He agreed to meet me.

"Director Jake McCarthy and Jack Lord, chair of the board's transportation committee, and I showed up about 7:30 the following morning at the bus stop and met all four Carusos for the first time.

"As we watched the bus come over the crown of the hill and pick up his sons, Mr. Caruso looked at me and said that maybe the bus stop wasn't so bad after all. He and his wife thanked us for coming, and we parted amicably. As far as I knew, Jonathan and Peter got the bus there until they finished high school.

"However, years later, after I'd retired, someone told me that a few days after that amicable parting, Mr. Caruso contacted the transportation office and, without my knowledge, arranged for his sons to be picked up on Newtown Road, just behind their house.

If this is true, it's consistent with what I learned in time about Rich Caruso: He rarely gave up. He just found another way.

"The next year, 1983, Peter was in 1st grade, Jonathan in third, and this time Caruso called, concerned about the size of Jonathan's class: twenty-three compared to the average of nineteen in all other grades. He asked me to add a 3rd-grade teacher to reduce class size. When I explained why I didn't feel it necessary to do so, Mr. Caruso asked if I'd meet him at Ithan School to discuss this in person rather than by phone.

"This was the same year the school board and I had closed two of Radnor's elementary schools because of low enrollment, leaving several empty classrooms in the two remaining schools, Ithan and Wayne. The following Wednesday night, I entered Ithan Elementary School and found myself meeting with Mr. Caruso and over thirty-five 3rd-grade parents in one of those empty classrooms.

"After an hour of discussion explaining why the enrollment bubble in 3rd grade required twenty-three students to a class, I assured the parents that the excellent teachers and strong curriculum meant their children would do equally well as those in other grades.

"Realizing I wasn't going to budge, Mr. Caruso pulled out his ace of spades: he'd give me all the money I needed to hire an additional 3rd-grade teacher, including benefits and professional development; I could place the teacher in one of the empty classrooms, bringing the average class size to eighteen.

"I declined his offer, explaining that in a high socioeconomic school system like Radnor, letting parents pay for special interests out of their own pockets could change the whole foundation of public education, not to mention open the door to advertising schemes, which I also had declined in the past.

"As we walked out of the building that night, Mr. Caruso invited me to come to his home to see the renovations they'd made to the stately old house. When my wife and I did visit his home, we saw oriental rugs, remarkable sculptures, and original works of art throughout the house. Later, I learned that some of the paintings were by Walter Baum, uncle of a man who had helped Richard Caruso develop his vision of what was possible.

"Over the next few years, differences between us on school issues continued to arise, but our communication remained cordial."

In addition to caring intensely about education, both Rich and Sally thought it was important to show their sons the world. No matter how busy life got, they made time for family vacations. Many people Rich worked with would later say things like, "Rich was always working: day, night, weekends. I never remember his taking time off." His grown sons would make jokes about their dad having his head at work while his body was with them on trips, but the family did take trips, many of them.

One of those trips wasn't for just the boys, though. The summer of 1984, Rich and Sally invited Dana and Bonnie, both sixteen then, to go to Italy with them and Jon, still nine, and Peter, seven. They got to stay in the homes of some of their relatives and got to know many cousins.

Peter was especially impressed later: "After our trip to Italy, two of our 'new' cousins, Frankie and Joey, showed up at our house for a visit. One day we took them out to a field to play soccer. I couldn't believe how good they were—it was amazing. When they grew up, both became dentists, and we kept in touch with them."

More than thirty years after the trip, Bonnie lit up remembering it: "That ended up being one of the most amazing trips I've ever been on. I will always be grateful to Rich and Sally for that trip. I learned so much about both sets of grandparents and where they came from."

Maybe his own grandparents' lives, simpler and closer to the land, had been an influence on Rich's unique version of luxury.

He lived in a spacious home with original paintings, and he climbed into ditches. He earned much more than he'd known was possible, and a vein of frugality ran throughout his life.

Ready to pay a teacher's annual salary for his sons' benefit, Rich also relished finding free meals for them during those early school years. Jonathan grinned, recalling, "Dad was very proud to take the family out every Saturday night to Rustler Steak House. We got to eat free! He got to treat his family and at the same time teach us to be fiscally responsible."

Rich taught his sons many other things too during their school years: lines from old movies, for one thing. When he'd worked in a theater during high school, the same films had played over and over and bored into Rich's brain. For decades, he could recite whole scenes of dialogue word for word. Jon and Peter thought that was kind of funny, but they probably got more out of his coaching them in baseball.

Both of them belonged to Little League teams when they were in 4th, 5th, and 6th grades. Rich would take turns coaching their teams: Jon's team one year, Peter's the next.

Peter remembered that his team won the league championship two years in a row and that "Dad drove a Cadillac Eldorado. After practice, instead of all the kids waiting for parents to pick them up, Dad would tell them to pile into his big Eldorado and take them home with us. They'd all play video games and wait for their parents to pick them up at our place. He thought that was more fun for them than waiting around to get picked up at practice. Two of the favorite games were Tetris and Space Invaders. Dad and I played those together."

It didn't go as well for Jonathan at first: "I didn't think I was good at baseball, but Dad insisted and became the coach. He would leave work early to coach us and to work with me at home on pitching. Usually he put me on first base, but one day he made me go out and be the pitcher. I said no, but he was unmoved and kept me in. Looking back on that, I realized it was a good thing because I was good at pitching, which he already knew. In several games, I pitched the first three innings. I went on to play in the international league. From his dog-headed insistence, I gained confidence in my pitching and realized I liked it."

The boys kept learning, and the large family kept growing. Rich's youngest sibling, Joe, had gotten married and had Cono's tenth and youngest grandchild, Kristin, who was a factor in her father and her Uncle Rich working together on a business deal several years later. Around that time too, Carmen's daughter, Bonnie, was thinking about what college major to pick and asked her father what Rich's had been. She followed his example and chose accounting too, as Rich had followed Coach Pittello's example: another form of mentoring perhaps, wordless and long-lasting.

Business kept growing as well. Rich and Jim Sullivan kept getting offers to buy the Rustler franchise—Collins Foods in California wanted to expand its Sizzler Steak House chains to the northeastern market by incorporating Rustler. It took a while and heralded changes for Rich: "We eventually accepted their offer. Tenly Enterprises was sold to Collins Foods in July 1985 at a large profit" for Rich, Jim, Carmen, Herb, and all the others who'd invested in the Rustler franchise.

Rich said, "Bill Marriott rehired Jim Sullivan, who spent the rest of his career there building and managing Marriott as a worldwide company. Jim and I had shared a very successful mentoring relationship, transitioning effortlessly between the roles of mentor and protégé, taking turns teaching and learning." Those years working together had been good ones for both of them on many levels.

There was another transition that year as well. In 1985, Cono died at ninety-one.

By the time he'd lost both parents, Rich was forty-two, married with children, successful in business, and wealthy by any measure. He'd helped and been helped by others, developed his own path and found he loved collaborating with others, had good friends and coworkers, and kept family ties strong—and yet, he felt something missing:

"Even having much success with Provco and Tenly through LFC, by 1985, after the sale of Rustler, I was having a hard time thinking of any substantive accomplishments other than financial success. What difference had I made?

"I had needed the money earned from my jobs before LFC and had learned a lot from each position held, but I didn't feel satisfied then either, wondering if I'd made any contributions to the larger world. Later, working at LFC, I'd found so much happiness in working with a team of people and developing a company in a positive way that often I didn't even think about getting paid.

"Still, though, I felt a desire to do something more, to make a difference for others. What was the bigger picture? I wanted to have a comprehensive understanding of personal success and share that understanding with others.

"I knew many years were left in my professional life. These first twenty years had been full of learning, had opened up the world to me, and they were over. What were my career goals for the next twenty? How could I make decisions within a framework that would bring this deeper satisfaction I kept wanting?

"As I asked myself these questions, slowly some answers came. In time, I laid out personal goals, nine things I wanted to accomplish. They became the criteria, the framework, for the rest of my career: standards for finding a new career path that would have a deeper impact on more people and standards for redefining my life."

RICHARD CARUSO'S NINE GOALS

1. Do something intellectually challenging.

2. Work with leading-edge technology.

3. Work with people I like and respect and who respect me.

4. Work on something that benefits all humanity.

5. Personally help make other people's dreams come true.

6. Accomplish something important that hasn't been done before.

7. Create a vision that others can understand and follow.

8. Create interesting career opportunities for others.

9. If all the criteria above are fulfilled, be financially successful. [*]

---

[*] See appendix 1 for a version of "Richard Caruso's Nine Goals" that can be copied and framed or displayed in your home or workplace.

CHAPTER 5

MAKING MENTORING
MAINSTREAM
1986 TO 1988

Some men are uncommon to extraordinary degree, others to lesser.
And perhaps most uncommon of all is the common man whose
achievements are exalted beyond the expectation of his circumstances.
—CRAWFORD H. GREENEWALT,
THE UNCOMMON MAN, 1959

R ich had been setting goals and wanting to make a difference since he was a boy. Did Cono's death in 1985 deepen
that need to help? Russell Baum's in 1979 certainly had.
As Rich administered funds in Baum's will, he wondered what he
wanted in his own. After taking care of family, what would he do
with the rest of all this wealth he'd accrued? How could he use
it to make a difference? "I was inspired by my own unlikely success
to search for a way to help others realize their personal ambitious
dreams" was how Rich put it.

As he searched, it grew increasingly clear to Rich that all along,
he'd been helped by others and by access to resources—usually just
when he most needed them. He wanted to give that same kind of
help to many others. How, though?

He pictured an organization: one that would last run by someone whose character had been tested and someone he trusted. By

then, Rich saw each person as unique and saw that uniqueness as important. What he'd create had to help each person reach his own vision of success, foster his own values. How did an organization do that?

By 1986, at forty-three, Rich had thought for years about all of this. He'd settled on nine goals for this next stage of his life and felt ready to act, so he called Dr. Crosby, who was getting ready to retire. This time, Rich asked him to lunch.

"Mr. Caruso, you've been a burr under my saddle for ten years. Are you sure you want to have lunch with me?" is what Crosby, born in rural Texas, replied.

His cleaned-up memory of Rich's response was "Dr. Crosby, I know I've been a pain in your side for ten years, but I like your style! You've always been accessible, always willing to listen to my concerns. You've been kind to me and respected my ideas even when we differed."

Because of the way Crosby handled conflicts between them over the years, Rich came to think of him as "an impressive individual." That wasn't enough, though. Rich wanted to hire Crosby for more than style, or accessibility, or even his rare ability to separate issues from individuals. Rich had done his homework: "Dr. John C. Crosby, superintendent of schools of the Radnor Township School District, was retiring after a thirty-year career in education, twenty years as superintendent in three Pennsylvania districts. During his twelve-year tenure in Radnor, the school district, its teachers, and its students earned national honors. The *Wall Street Journal* named Radnor High School one of the top ten in the US, and *Consumer Reports* rated the school district one of the nation's best. President Reagan had invited Dr. Crosby to a White House event recognizing outstanding educators." Crosby's resume checked out. "I wanted John to become involved in this venture because he was an expert in education. I wanted him to find the best way possible for individuals to learn from each other in order to accomplish their goals."

Rich wanted that and more. Throughout his prominent career in education, Crosby nurtured and nudged administrators, teachers, and students toward excellence. Many of them became outstanding educators, principals, superintendents, professors, business executives, and leaders in their communities. Five of his six assistant superintendents became superintendents, and many colleagues and students distinguished themselves in illustrious careers.

In other words, Dr. Crosby had done for people around him what others had done for Rich. Now could he find ways to do that on a larger scale?

Soon after that call, Rich and John Crosby met for lunch in a small restaurant near LFC. Rich told John about his background: Italian immigrant parents, meager means as a boy, at forty-three wealthy beyond imagination. That was due, Rich said, to help from dozens of people, but four men stood out in his mind. They'd given him advice and resources at crucial points, *and* they'd cared about his dreams and values. Coach John Boyd, Coach Jim Garrett, Coach Bob Pittello, and Russell Baum had seen not only what Rich could become but also what he wanted to become. They'd helped him grow toward what truly mattered to *him*.

Then Rich got specific: "I want to start with a million dollars to have you build a nonprofit foundation that does for others what those four men did for me."

"But what does that mean?" John asked.

The reply was pure Rich: "I don't know, but I think you can do it."

He added, "I've thrown money at problems without success before, so you don't have to make money or raise it. You do have to provide a service to others. They can pay according to their ability, or your services can be free."

Rich did have a specific name in mind, though: "Recently I read *The Uncommon Man*, a book by Crawford Greenewalt, retired president of DuPont. I felt inspired by it and want to call our organization the Uncommon Man Foundation."

"Mr. Caruso, we can't call it that," John said, accepting this challenge—now they were a "we." John's directness and humor came with him. So did discernment gained from life with an equal-partner wife and an accomplished daughter already showing the relatable grit that would land her at the top of her field. He added, "We'll have to change one word. We'll call it the Uncommon *Individual* Foundation."

Rich set John up in a tiny cubicle near his own office at LFC, and the brand new executive director of the Uncommon Individual Foundation (UIF) began figuring out how to elicit and nurture the uncommon individual that Rich believed was within every single person.

First came research to define the foundation's mission. Early on, John came across a newspaper article about multimillionaire Eugene Lang, born in New York of immigrant parents about a generation before Rich. In 1981, Lang had been asked to speak to sixty-one 6th graders graduating from P.S. 121 in East Harlem, where he'd graduated fifty years earlier. He'd planned the usual work-hard-to-succeed talk until the principal whispered to him on the way to the podium that, typically, three-quarters of the school's students didn't finish high school—so Lang made an impromptu change to his speech. After telling the students about witnessing Dr. Martin Luther King Jr.'s famous "I Have a Dream" speech at the 1963 March on Washington, he urged them to dream their own dreams, and then he made a promise to every single student in the class: "If you will graduate from high school, I will pay your way through college."

Next, he went home and set up the I Have a Dream Foundation. Yes, he'd pay their college tuition, but to help them get through high school so they could use that tuition, he'd also provide an extensive program of tutoring, guidance, and *mentoring*.

The word *mentoring* jumped off the page   a word rarely seen or heard in the mid-1980s. John showed the article to Rich, who agreed: *mentoring* was exactly the word they'd been searching for to describe what they were trying to do. Theirs would be, as far as they knew, the first nonprofit foundation devoted exclusively to mentoring.

It must be not just the first but also, Rich stipulated, the gold standard for such programs. He told John to produce steps for creating a successful mentoring program with a curriculum that could be tailored to the needs of any group.

They began reading everything on mentoring they could find. When John saw a full-page ad in *Newsweek* on Dow Chemical's science program for at-risk students in Chicago, he showed the ad to Rich, found the program's head, and accepted Charles Infante's invitation to visit Dow's office in Midland, Michigan.

As John remembered it, "Rich and I had several meetings with the president and members of his leadership team. They were wonderful hosts and shared their philosophy of helping others through science education. Then we shared our idea of using mentoring to help others develop their full potential, and I'll never forget what Dow's president exclaimed: 'Oh, you're trying to have happen by design what has always happened by accident!'"

As they dug into resources on mentoring, Rich and John jotted down names of persons running the few mentoring programs that existed nationwide in colleges, corporations, and businesses. By 1988, when that list got to fifteen, Rich remembered, "We invited them to participate in a three-day mentoring symposium so we could better understand what they were doing and how they defined *mentoring*. The foundation held the symposium at American College in Bryn Mawr, Pennsylvania, and paid expenses for the fifteen 'mentoring experts.'"

Over the course of the weekend, Rich became especially close to Dr. Thomas P. Land, head of the mentoring program at Motorola. They stayed in touch and later worked together in a way that benefitted both of them. That happened all the time in business, of course, and was a familiar pattern in Rich's life by then. He'd noticed it and thought about it. Maybe he'd read that it was "good business." Networking was touted as good strategy, and huge rolodexes like Rich's were common.

Some business students hear advice about networking as a way to advance self-interest: "Meet lots of people and be nice to them so you can access them for help later." As their awareness grows, some people perceive self-interest in a more nuanced way: "Meet lots of people and be nice to them because what you send out comes back to you in time." Possibly Rich tried out both of those layers of meaning, but he seemed to come at the whole mutual-benefit idea from an even deeper place.

Maybe part of his perspective was that he found his way to gratitude early on. Belonging, health, food, clothes, a home, schooling, religious/spiritual grounding: the basics had been there for Rich. Still, he had friends who were given extras too, and he'd had to find ways to get those on his own. He'd had to share his busy parents' scarce attention with two and then three siblings. He could have felt shortchanged, felt that anything extra given to him was his due, but he didn't. He noticed when the nuns gave him the chance to be an altar boy, and he saw it as a gift. He paid attention when Coach Boyd offered him a path to college, and he'd felt grateful. He'd been aware, even then, of the interest, advice, referrals, housing, and trust Russell Baum had given him. Was this habit of feeling grateful related to his wanting to give?

When he'd bought ice cream for friends after selling papers on the boardwalk, maybe, at ten, all he'd felt was the fun of feeling popular, but he'd noticed that good feeling and remembered it. He'd paid for Henry Haines's ski trips now and then because he'd wanted to, not to get anything back. Giving to Fran "was in his heart." Helping struggling start-ups reach goals felt *fun* to him. Did his satisfaction in helping others come from the gratitude he felt for the help he'd been given?

Psychologists write that one basic human need is to contribute. Somehow, Rich got in touch with that need and then, characteristically, dug deeper. He came to think that wanting to help others was in us all, and he wanted to foster it.

The *Philadelphia Inquirer* extensively covered the symposium on mentoring, which ended with dinner for more than a hundred people. Next came studying the presentations: What could Rich and John learn from them?

Each of the talks defined mentoring as a one-to-one, top-down relationship: an assigned mentor represented the organization's objectives and helped each protégé (mentee) meet a high level of performance. As protégés became more effective at their jobs, they helped the organization reach its goals.

That confirmed what Rich and John had culled from the few articles on mentoring they'd found so far. Searching more, they became convinced that all types of groups can benefit from good mentoring programs. Then they teased out what those specific benefits were. Mentoring helps organizations improve how they

- train new employees,
- transmit institutional knowledge and culture,
- attract new employees,

- grow and maintain a diverse workforce,
- assess performance and potential of employees,
- assign employees to projects,
- promote employees, and
- foster a culture of positive reciprocity, support, and cooperation that spreads beyond the organization.

These findings would help them explain the value of mentoring to businesses, civic groups, and others. That was a start, but it seemed incomplete.

Most mentoring programs focused on the goals of their organizations. Most organizations thought that they could achieve their goals best by fostering the *professional* development of their employees or members. That meant participants benefitted most if their passions were aligned with the organization's goals—but what if they weren't?

A few mentoring programs did try to help participants reach personal goals. The top goal of many mentees was promotion to higher-level position and pay within the organization, so as they did well, the organization did too. At times, though, a mentoring-program participant took a job outside the organization. Rather than being upset, the organization usually had enough long-range vision to be happy that it had been part of the individual's growth and even to stay connected informally—to count it, still, as a success.

That certainly fit Rich's underlying vision of helping others as he'd been helped, to move toward his own goals in his own way. When Russell Baum had suggested to him four free years of college at West Point, Rich had thought about it but declined. Free would have been easier, but he knew he needed flexibility more than financial ease. Now helping people in a way that let them be true to themselves was the kind of help he wanted to give.

At that point, sharing Rich's vision and using what they'd learned so far, John outlined a process for the Uncommon Individual Foundation to use in bringing mentoring to groups.[*] Their skeleton program would last nine to twelve months with most groups and would look something like this:

a. The organization sets up a steering committee and program head to establish goals that balance the needs of all participants.

b. Mentors and mentees either volunteer for or apply to the program.

c. The committee and its coordinator, with UIF guidance, match each mentee to a mentor.

d. UIF provides training for all involved, ideally throughout the duration of the program.

e. At the end of the program, the committee and UIF hold a luncheon celebration at which several mentoring pairs share their experience.

f. UIF evaluates the program in order to determine its benefits, figure out ways to improve future programs, and share its findings with the committee.

This outline seemed simple and flexible enough to use for mentoring programs in businesses, schools, and nonprofits. It was one of the straight-edge pieces of the puzzle they were putting together,

---

[*] See appendix 2, "Ten Steps for Establishing a Corporate (Structured) Mentoring Program," for Dr. Crosby's fuller development of this list.

but it also had to fit Rich's "3-D–chess mind." Both Rich and John thought in layers of meaning and were used to excavating. No one who knew them both was surprised that their understanding of mentoring kept growing.

They found examples of mentoring even in religious texts. In the Judeo-Christian tradition, both Old and New Testaments tell stories of mentoring. The Hebrew word *rabbi*, "my master," has come to mean "revered teacher," a person to ask for wise guidance. Jesus's disciples saw him as a mentor who shared teachings while answering their questions. Buddhist, Confucian, and Islamic writings describe mentoring in their own words. A common thread in most all these examples is of one-way help, a mentor or teacher helping a protégé or seeker: the same pattern Rich and John had found so far in existing programs.

It was when Rich and John remembered how "mentor" entered our language that they uncovered another layer. In Homer's ancient epic *The Odyssey*, its hero Odysseus, before leaving his wife and infant son Telemachus to go fight in the Trojan War, asked his friend *Mentor* to protect and guide Telemachus while Odysseus was away—for maybe a year or two, he thought. Mentor filled that role faithfully for the next twenty years, definitely earning his way into our dictionaries as the definition of "wise and trusted counselor."

The definition lasted, but the story gave a richer picture: Telemachus had had multiple mentors. So had Rich. So had John. How could they use this knowledge to help the next generation, and the next, and the next?

They'd been thinking UIF would train mentors to guide mentees. Should they instead provide several mentors for each mentee? How had Rich and John been helped by many people? Rich knew his own history. Was John's anything like his? Were there common threads they could learn from?

John grew up on a dust-bowl cotton farm in West Texas, where hard work, honesty, and perseverance weren't just values but requirements for living in a farming community and surviving physically. By nine, John was driving a tractor and hoeing cotton, often dawn to dusk. He fed chickens and slopped hogs. He noticed how animals cared for their young and taught survival skills to the next generation. He saw horses and cows shade each other from the Texas sun. Animals mentored each other and him. The land itself was a mentor; if he and his family learned its lessons, they could eke a living from it.

Sometimes in such environments, learning how to stay alive crowds out other learning, but John had an equally powerful mentor in his mother. She was a schoolteacher and self-taught Bible scholar. He learned to love reading the books his mother first read aloud, learned to write and draw and sing, followed her example by attending college, and majored in English instead of agriculture.

His farmer father, a master carpenter, was just as powerful a mentor. John's drawing skills came from this man who envisioned a finished product and then created it, who designed the church building his family attended three times a week and then built it with help from other farmers.

Building a church required collaboration that didn't take others' actions personally. Seeing people on the work crew often, in their small church weekly, and on each other's farms in emergencies: all of that made looking for the best in others not a high-minded virtue but a necessary skill. One family living alone in windswept West Texas rarely thrived. The church, salt-of-the-earth neighbors, and close community mentored John in ways that served him well.

When Rich wanted a special school bus pick-up for his sons, when he'd filled a classroom with parents insisting on a smaller class size, John may have felt some irritation or frustration, but turning people with different ideas into enemies wasn't a strategy he'd learned. Problems presented had to be addressed and solved, but the people bringing up problems were just people, more or less like him. Judging and name-calling didn't work in the long run. Their little church would never have gotten finished if his father had criticized those helping him: have the worker fix the work if needed, but respect the man. You'd see those folks again. You'd need each other. Let's figure this out.

John's life had been filled with mentors whom he hadn't always noticed at the time but remembered later. So had Rich's. They wondered why. As they worked together and shared stories, Rich and John found surprising parallels in their city-kid/country-boy lives. In 5th grade, John had saved the money he made from growing cotton and used it to buy himself bedroom furniture. After 6th grade, Rich had saved money from summer jobs to buy his first dog. When Rich had wanted ice cream, he'd shined shoes to buy it. When John had learned that he was allergic to cow's milk, he had bought, fed, and milked three nanny goats and drunk their milk until he left for college.

When their parents had said, "No, we won't get that for you," neither Rich nor John had heard, "You can't have this." Instead, both had heard, "You can have this if you figure out how." Both had gotten very good at figuring out how. Both had gotten very good at searching out resources. Was that part of mentoring too? What did the mentee have to do with this whole mentoring thing they were delving into? Had they been looking at it upside down?

Then there was this other piece, another pattern both Rich and John had noticed in their lives. When they really had dug in, worked hard, creatively scrounged resources no one else had seen, kept on past tired, done more than anyone else thought they could—then, over and over, what they needed showed up.

Coach Garrett had gotten Rich the scholarship he'd needed to attend Susquehanna. At Abilene Christian College, John's band director, Professor Douglas Fry, had gotten John a scholarship he had to have to stay in school. At Bucknell, a professor had taken Rich on as his assistant, a key piece Rich needed to get his graduate degree. At Vanderbilt's Peabody College, Dr. James Colmey fostered John's interest in school administration and encouraged him to move to the northeast to work and attend Columbia's Teacher's College, where Professor Felix McCormick gave John the part-time job and full scholarship he had to have to earn his EdD—well, until he seemed to hit a brick wall.

John was nearly through with his doctoral dissertation and needed only recent census numbers to finish but found that those numbers wouldn't be made public for three more years. That's when, over Christmas with his wife's family in rural Tennessee, as they visited an old friend there, John mentioned the impasse and was overheard by the friend's father. Then US congressman Joe L. Evins, "Mr. Joe" as John called him, quietly left the room and phoned the director of the US Census Bureau. After about fifteen minutes, he returned and told John the bureau would make those data available to him. Mr. Joe then reached into his pocket and handed John the key to his home in Washington, saying he could stay as long as he needed to get the data.

This was reminiscent of the summer Russell Baum let Rich live in his home to attend summer school after Rich missed a college semester. In both cases, someone they hadn't known long gave them the piece they needed to keep moving toward a goal they'd worked on as hard as they knew how.

Henry Haines said of Rich, "He was lucky that way." John's mother would have said John was "blessed." Whatever this "when you've done all you can" kind of help was called, both Rich and

John shared the sense that it was a factor in the mentoring puzzle they were putting together.

Giving to others the kinds of help he'd been given felt important to Rich, so showing mentors when and how to help mentees remained important. What part did the mentees play in the relationship, though?

Rich hadn't expected help, was used to doing for himself, had learned to take calculated risks but not mourn very long over the ones that didn't work. He'd heard the American truism, "80 percent of success is never giving up." John had grown up hearing, "Stick with the haying 'til the haying's done." Eventually, Rich's favorite became a Japanese saying, "Fall seven, rise eight." Did living your life in that never-give-up way somehow attract help?

Rich and John knew words wouldn't be enough to help mentees embody this quality, but figuring out a way to teach it seemed essential. For now, they'd stick with Rich's first answer to the whole puzzle: they didn't know, but they thought they could do it. They'd keep figuring it out as they went along.

What they knew so far was that

- mentoring benefits groups that use it,
- mentoring benefits mentees and mentors,
- mentees/protégés usually have many mentors, and
- the mentee's dream or goal is central to the process.

They also had a flexible outline for bringing the benefits of mentoring into any kind of group, so they began—and as they worked, they kept learning.

Over time, John became aware of a pattern in the interpersonal relationships that developed in all the groups using mentoring. Studying it, he found four distinct steps in the typical progression of a mentoring relationship:

1. **Mutual Admiration**: Mentors and protégés start by seeking approval, putting their best foot forward, and presenting a positive image. *John came to call this the "sparkle phase." Its shiny newness was balanced by the anxiety that both Rich and John remember feeling with some mentors early on: "Trying to make a favorable impression," Rich wrote, "wanting a deeper, more honest relationship," while afraid the less-than-best parts of themselves might be judged lacking.*

2. **The Developing Relationship**: As trust and mutual respect grow and they begin to share confidences, the mentor moves into giving the protégé advice and help, guiding more of the conversation. *Rich remembers feeling that Russell Baum was in charge of their talks at this stage, doing most of the giving and supporting, and Rich listened more. John thinks of the first time he worked as an assistant to a strict but supportive superintendent and how he relaxed more in this phase as they began achieving common goals.*

3. **Achieving Goals**: As the protégé begins using the mentor's advice and the mentor gives more on-target advice based on understanding the protégé's dreams better, some goals are reached and some are modified. The relationship becomes a bit more relaxed and often more resilient. If emotional and communication skills are fostered, the mentor and protégé are better able to let disagreements arise in this phase and work through them together. *Rich describes the pair in this phase as being "less cautious with and more realistic about each other," slowly moving from a top-down relationship toward a more mutual one. John also saw in this stage seeds of the next one—as he achieved established goals, his mentor gave less direction, so a natural pulling-away began.*

4. **Breaking Away**: In this last stage, both clear achievements and a now resource-rich environment affirm the protégé's sense of self-reliance. That sense of independence leads naturally to the process of disengaging from the mentor as a source of advice. The pair moves toward either terminating their relationship or transforming it into a more equal one, sometimes becoming lifelong friends. *Rich remembers many of his former mentors becoming friends for the rest of his life. He also faced what happens at times: "Some mentors feel resentful if they believe they weren't given appropriate credit for their help or perceive their protégé's accomplishments as overshadowing their own. Most often, though, mentors feel proud of having contributed to their protégé's success," as Rich did when his nephew Jerry became CEO of Provco Group. John values the lifelong friendship of the first superintendent he worked for and feels proud knowing that five of his six assistant superintendents during a span of twenty years became outstanding superintendents.*

Articulating this pattern gave UIF another tool to use in nurturing mentoring programs for all sorts of groups. John knew of research on developmental stages in other kinds of relationships (friendships, marriages, work partners, groups, etc.) but hadn't come across such findings on mentoring pairs.

Having this knowledge was a piece of UIF's uniqueness. It also gave John and Rich more to learn: How to increase the number of mentors who find lasting satisfaction in their sharing. How pairs can copy the DNA model of moving apart and coming back together at a higher level. How to support the necessary "breaking away" stage as a help-going-one-way partnership grows into a mutual one. There was always more to learn, and learning more was UIF's hallmark.

The Mentoring Relationship

1) *Mutual Admiration:* Protégés and mentors try to make a favorable impression. This is known as the "sparkle phase"

2) *The Developing Relationship:* Mentors lead the conversation in the beginning, eventually becoming the supporter after mutual trust is built.

3) *Achieving Goals:* Relationship gets strongenr after establishing understanding of one another. Achievement of goals may cause natural disengagement from one another.

4) *Breaking Away:* Participants' growth and development may lead to mutual termination of the alliances, while other relationships continue on for years or more.

John called this the Life Cycle of the Mentoring Relationship.

Another key to UIF's effectiveness was that Rich and John shifted focus to the protégé as the central figure in the duo. They discovered two vital facts:

1. Most persons who succeed, in any definition of that term, access multiple mentoring resources over the course of their lives, whether they realize it or not, and

2. Protégés frequently assume leadership roles in their mentoring relationships in order to pursue objectives they define for themselves—it is, after all, their own development at stake!

These were two essential threads in the mentoring tapestry. Then they found a third:

3. Successful protégés surround themselves with a variety of resources, creating a personal mentor-rich environment that Rich named the *mentorsphere*. It's a vital, fluid sphere. As protégés build on past mentoring experiences, they continually recreate a mix of supports to fit new ventures and their own growth.

These subtler aspects of mentoring had been hiding in plain sight, needing to be brought to awareness so they could be taught and used purposely.

As Rich and John kept refining the foundation's understanding of mentoring, the classical Mentor-to-Telemachus image became only one facet of the mentorsphere they provided. Both mentors and protégés increasingly thrived in the array of relationships and resources UIF brought to their programs.

Later, they noticed yet another nuance: most protégés shift between the roles of protégé and mentor over and over again in their lives, giving-receiving-giving: "Like an electric current," UIF trainers would in time describe it, "traveling both ways. Sometimes both of you, mentor and protégé, will look at each other and ask, 'Are you the mentor now, or am I?'"

Over time, it became apparent that most protégés had to live this back-and-forth pattern to be comfortable in it, so another of UIF's strengths came to be providing situations in which protégés could experience and practice that full range of roles in the mentoring dance.

Although both Rich and John had experienced mentoring throughout their lives, studying and sharing it heightened their understanding of its impact on personal happiness and success. One summary Rich gave was as follows:

> The key to effective mentoring is the protégé's passion, which inspires mentors to invest their time and energy, which strengthens the protégé's determination, which propels protégés to exceed their own expectations.

He could state the foundation's mission clearly by then:

> The goal of the Uncommon Individual Foundation is to educate people on how to engage the power of mentoring so as to help themselves and others to achieve success as each individual defines it.

This intense and ongoing work brought to Rich's life a coherence that he had yearned for. The nine goals he'd struggled to articulate made plain his need to live a life of meaning. This organization he and John were shaping was adhering to those goals, providing the meaning he now insisted on. His understanding of life had grown. He wrote, "Even the most primal human impulse, survival, is rarely possible without cooperation." It's a quiet statement, easy to overlook. Rich had succeeded in business by anyone's definition of success. They say that business is all about competition, and Rich had certainly *won* at that game. Somehow, though, he'd held onto this core value within himself: cooperation.

Then he went further: "The history of human innovation and achievement suggests that humans are predisposed to helping one another." This basic human need to contribute, which he saw as part of himself and everyone else, underlay the Uncommon Individual Foundation he and John had birthed. Now it was out in the open.

Rich's understanding, that we humans are built to help each other, would seem radical to some, but he'd embodied it now. He felt freer.

"Until this time, the world thought I was more successful than I actually felt because our society measures success by wealth and prestige. With the establishment of this foundation, though, I'd created a tangible realization of the nine criteria for business that I'd laid out for myself and of the meaning I'd found for my own life. Then I felt truly personally successful."

Frances and Richard Caruso
In front of their house
Atlantic City, New Jersey

Frances, Louise holding
Joseph, and Richard
2314 Leopold Terrace
Atlantic City, New Jersey

Richard Caruso
First grade
St. Michael's Grammar School
Atlantic City, New Jersey

Richard Caruso
First Communion
Second grade
St. Michael's Grammar School
Atlantic City, New Jersey

Richard Caruso
High school graduation
1961
Atlantic City High School

Russell Baum
In front of his home
Where Richard lived while
attending St. Joe's
Between his freshman and
sophomore years—Summer 1962
Latches Lane
Merion Station, Pennsylvania

Richard Caruso, guard
All Conference, All State, 1962–1965
SU's five-year record 40-3-1, 1960-1965
Susquehanna University
Selinsgrove, Pennsylvania

Richard and Sally Caruso
Wedding—August 5, 1972
In the garden of Sally's
prerevolutionary home
It had been in her family
for six generations
Poconos
Snydersville, Pennsylvania

Richard and Sally with his parents
"Louisa" (as the family called her) and Cono
Wedding in beautiful garden arbor at Sally's home
(Reception was at Penn Stroud Hotel—Stroudsburg, Pennsylvania)

Richard, Frances, Joe, and Carmen with their parents
At a birthday celebration for their mother

Rich and Sally with
Jonathan,
Christened in
Sally's family's
christening gown
1974
Brother Peter would
wear the same
christening gown

Richard holding Jonathan
At their first home
Sweet Briar Road
King of Prussia, Pennsylvania

Richard and Sally
1975, before Peter was born
Lucerne, Switzerland

Uncle Rich and
Jerry Holtz
Seventh grade, 1975-76
At Caruso grandparents'
home
Margate, New Jersey

Sally, Jonathan, Peter, and Richard
Family trip to Italy
1984
The Roman Forum

Jonathan, Peter, and Sally
Visiting relatives
In Italy

Peter and Sally
With dog Coco
Third grade, 1985-86
Villanova home

Jonathan, Richard, and Peter
At Caruso grandparents' home
Margate, New Jersey

Peter, Richard, Sally, and Jonathan
Jonathan's trip to Western United States

Peter Caruso
Playing football
Fourth Grade, 1986-87
St. Thomas's Catholic Youth
Organization

Sally, Jonathan, and Richard
Playing Football
Seventh Grade, 1987-88
Radnor Middle School
Wayne, Pennsylvania

Peter, Richard,
Jonathan, and Sally
Weekend before Christmas
Family room
Villanova, Pennsylvania

Uncle Rich and Dana
Dana and Chris Conner's wedding day
December 13, 1997

Richard
At home
November 12, 2005
Villanova, Pennsylvania

Coach Pittello, Richard Caruso, and Head Coach Garrett
Mentors and friends since college
Susquehanna University

Richard, on right, with Jay Leno, MC at the award ceremony
2006 Entrepreneur of the Year USA
Palm Springs, California

Richard and Sally Caruso
At the party following
the award ceremony
2006 Entrepreneur of the Year USA
Palm Springs, California

Richard and Sally
Second place award
2007 Entrepreneur of the
Year International
Monte Carlo

Peter Arduini, Stuart Essig, and Richard Caruso
Integra LifeSciences celebrating twenty years on NASDAQ

Jerry Holtz and Gary DeLella
The Provco Group
2018
Villanova, Pennsylvania

Richard Caruso and John Crosby
UIF President and Executive Director
Mentoring Symposium
October 1988
American College
Bryn Mawr, Pennsylvania

Richard Caruso and John Crosby
Still mentoring mentors
March 2016
Uncommon Individual Foundation
Devon, Pennsylvania

CHAPTER 6

STEPPING BACK TO GO FORWARD

1988 TO 1990

Our own fate is tied to each other, all over the world.
—JONATHAN CARUSO

T hen Rich went back to school.
While he and John were beginning the UIF in 1986, LFC was morphing into a whole new identity. Rich's mind played on both of those levels and—no surprise—came up with a third project as well.

In the 1980s, more businesses got into the kind of leasing LFC had done for a decade, but most weren't structured as well as it was and lost money. The company kept flourishing until the Tax Reform Act of 1986 reduced tax benefits associated with equipment leasing, making it less profitable. So LFC transitioned out of the leasing business and into other fields. One was alternative energy, including geothermal, wind, hydroelectric, and gas-fired regeneration.

Rich was wary of too much risk and advised moving into energy with caution. Others at LFC wanted to move faster while at the same time adding traditional energy sources—oil and gas—into the mix as well. Ultimately, the board backed the views of those wanting to stay in energy and focus on the alternative kinds. Rich, ever a team player, agreed to stay involved and help, but it wasn't his thing.

The 1986 tax law had changed the horse business too. Most people who'd been in it for tax reasons sold their interest. Their horse-breeding partnership dissolved in 1987, but Rich and Sally retained ownership of some horses, keeping them at the farm with Jeff Robbins for a while. For years they kept one horse in training, racing it at Philadelphia Park. They enjoyed naming their own racing stable: Fleur de Lis, which they associated with the Medici family in Florence, Italy. They designed their stable's jockey silks in purple and yellow with a large fleur-de-lis on the back.

JJ's Joy was a horse the whole family loved, and Rich and Sally raced him for six years. JJ won more than $200,000 for them. His usual style of racing was to drop back to last place in the beginning of a race and then make a big run in the stretch to the finish line. Jeff remembered one period when JJ got into a three-race streak of coming in second: "One day after his third time in second place, JJ was running again at Philadelphia Park. Before that race, Rich and Sally and I were with him and the jockey in the saddling enclosure. This time, Rich decided that JJ needed some coaching. He looked JJ in the eye and told him that in the last three races there'd always been one horse left in front of him at the finish line. 'This time,' Rich told him, 'have *no* horses in front of you when you get to the finish line.' The message must have gotten through because JJ came from last place, passed every horse in front of him, and won the race." That's when Jeff dubbed Rich "horse whisperer."

Jeff was a lauded trainer partly because he watched the behavior of horses so closely—well, horses *and* humans. He also watched how Rich bet: "Rich and Sally liked coming to the races to watch the horses. Rich enjoyed reading the daily racing form and analyzing each horse's past performance. He took great care and deliberated thoughtfully before picking which horse to bet on. Then he'd go up to the window and, just as with all of his financial transactions, always serious, buy everyone with him a $2 ticket for that race."

Once David had said about his Uncle Rich, "When he saw something that was humorous to him, his laugh was 89 percent his big smile." Jeff homed in on Rich's humor too—especially how much he liked to tell jokes on himself: "One day at the races, Rich was sitting outside on a bench reading the racing form when another man sat down and said, 'Hey, Rich, who do you like in the next race?' Rich was taken aback because he didn't recognize the man and was trying to figure out how this guy knew his name. It took Rich a minute to realize that he was wearing something Jeff had given him: a jacket with 'Rich' embroidered across the front! When he got the joke, everyone around him got a big laugh too. Rich had a great sense of humor and loved telling stories like that."

While enjoying the horses, helping as needed with LFC's energy projects, and keeping in touch with how John Crosby was developing UIF, Rich was also looking for a new direction: one that felt meaningful to him *and* fit his nine criteria. He'd kind of liked science in college, and he'd learned a bit about repairing medical devices when in the Army Reserve twenty years earlier. Now, for some reason, he felt drawn back to the medical field. So, being Rich, he created one more corporation to add to the hundred or so already part of LFC: LFC LifeSciences. He wasn't sure where this would lead, but it would have to achieve some of his goals—maybe especially the one about benefitting humanity.

While that was getting started, Rich was going to study in more depth this whole "helping-people-help-people" concept that he'd had hanging around in his head most of his life, the one he and John now called *mentoring*.

Not long after that, Rich made one of his periodic calls to stay in touch with Bill Muir. Rich told Bill that he'd been accepted to PhD programs at Wharton and Penn and some other universities but that all of them required two years of coursework, not to mention the dissertation. "Too long," Rich said.

Later, Rich made a call that Jim Sullivan had not expected: "One night, Rich called me and told me that he'd enrolled both of us in the doctoral program at the London School of Economics, had rented a flat for us, and paid the first year's tuition!" It might have been tempting, an adventure, but Jim had four very young children by then. The timing just wasn't good. Rich would go by himself. In 1988, he moved some clothes into the flat in London near Hyde Park and began work toward a PhD in mentoring and its uses in developing both individuals and organizations.

Rich would mine mentoring, and John would keep building the foundation: "We agreed that John would proceed with our original plans. Using the general steps we'd put together based on our research so far, he would design and implement structured mentoring programs with profit and nonprofit organizations interested in using mentoring." To get started, John would

- organize the programs,
- develop the curriculum,
- write training manuals,
- train mentors and protégés, and
- evaluate the mentoring process.

They'd keep an open dialogue. Rich wanted to study in depth the ideas that had kept coming up in the past two years as he and John had read and talked about mentoring. What about the protégé's role? What about the experiences he and John had grown up with: accessing help from many people, many resources? That went way beyond just assigning a mentor to a newbie. How could they design all aspects of mentoring into their program? Also, how could they convince organizations that mentoring, especially their particular take on mentoring, was worth a try? Saying "we just think so" might not be enough. It wasn't enough for Rich at any rate.

They'd start with "structured mentoring," the one-on-one, top-down kind, letting UIF begin in a way familiar to corporations and other organizations. If Rich came back with academic studies showing that more protégé-centered mentoring had value, John wouldn't be surprised. Others would feel more comfortable trying a now-evidence-based new way, and John would have some field-tested experience to build on. Then he'd adapt their Plan A in ways Rich's research suggested. It was an adventure, but a pretty organic one.

Ever proactive, Rich, after UIF's mentoring symposium, had followed up with Motorola's Thomas Land and gotten his agreement: Rich would use Motorola's mentoring program for his research. That piece was in place.

About every two weekends, Rich flew back to LFC's Radnor office to meet in person with the small team he'd assembled to work on the medical start-up he had in mind, to touch base with John if needed, and to see his family.

It was a tricky time for Sally. She relied heavily on her parents to help fill some of the gaps Rich's absence left. They came over often, usually every weekend Rich was gone. Later, Sally said that she couldn't have gotten through that period without her parents' help.

Jonathan was in 8th and 9th grades during Rich's commuting-from-London period. Peter was in 6th and 7th. They were probably old enough to understand why he was gone and not blame themselves for his absence as younger children are likely to do. They might even have noticed the value their dad put on lifelong learning. Still, research says children do better with both parents around. Rich did what he could to stay connected with his sons on the weekends he was home and on their family vacations.

Jonathan explained that earlier their dad had told them, "'Each of you pick a place you want to visit, and we'll go there in these next few years.' My mom picked Germany and Switzerland. My brother picked Asia. I picked the West, and my dad had picked Italy. On each trip, we were gone over a month. We toured the whole area of each place we visited, cities and countryside. We stopped along the way, saw things up close, and met people."

Although Peter was the one who'd chosen Asia, Jon seemed especially attuned to it: "We toured China before it had opened much to the West. Many people there hadn't seen Westerners, and my mom's blonde hair was fascinating to them; they'd reach out and touch it. Later, when Tiananmen Square happened, I knew exactly where it was. The temples in Thailand were amazing and everywhere. In Tokyo, when we were playing an arcade game called 1942, Dad thought it was funny because we, *and* the Japanese kids playing with us, were oblivious to the history behind it."

By the time he'd become a father himself, Jonathan had clearly absorbed some of his parents' core values. He spoke of the need for teaching financial literacy in high schools, of the importance of lifelong learning in and out of the classroom, of how much he wanted his own children to love learning. As if an afterthought, he added, "Our own fate is tied to each other, all over the world." It was a belief that seemed a corollary to his father's view of our universal human need to make life better for others. Family trips may have helped make up for Rich's time away from home. Apparently they brought other gifts too.

Those times with family gave Rich respite as well. During the other eleven months of those two years, he'd take courses, read, study, write, commute, repeat.

One of the reasons Rich had been so interested in Thomas Land's mentoring program at Motorola was that, although it had the usual structured setup, Land himself encouraged his employees to also engage in what Rich termed "natural mentoring." That's exactly what Rich wanted to get at: how the two were different, what effects each had, maybe even how to help both work on purpose. Could he compare the two and get enough data for a dissertation?

He could, and he did. Within two years, he had completed all coursework, designed and carried out the research project, and written and defended his dissertation.

It was titled "An Examination of Organizational Mentoring: The Case of Motorola." In it, he first looked at how much help protégés in the structured program wanted, tried to get, and thought they got from their assigned mentors. Overall, most thought they got some help but not as much as they wanted from mentors the program had paired them with.

Then Rich used his study to ask a second question: How much help did protégés get from assigned mentors *compared with* help they got from other persons and resources, help they ferreted out for themselves? It turned out that protégés saw other sources of mentoring as *more* important than the help from their officially assigned mentor—*significantly more*, Rich's statistics said.

He suggested that this unassigned help may not have been found in mentoring programs studied before because previous studies on mentoring hadn't asked that second question—so why had he? Cono's shoe-polish tins and brushes had been around the house for all of Rich's siblings to see, but only he had turned them into a way to make money for ice cream. At Price Waterhouse, all the accountants must have known of clients that were start-ups. Was Rich the only one who asked to be assigned to one? Of course he thought a protégé's initiative and dreams were significant; they had been in his life.

In Rich's words, "It was clear that structured mentoring is important and yields excellent results, but obviously it represented only a small part of mentoring because I'd mentored and been mentored throughout my life and had never been in a formal mentoring program." He was immersed in both research on and theories about mentoring during those years in London. He examined it from many angles and brought back clearer, more nuanced understandings to inform UIF's work. A few were as follows:

- If structured mentoring is working, it almost always evolves into natural mentoring; it's necessary to encourage both kinds of relationships.
- Protégés get help in professional as well as personal growth, which mutually reinforce each other in any kind of mentoring.
- Mentors don't share a defined set of qualifications. Most effective mentors seem to be knowledgeable, available, and willing to help; listen to and understand professional challenges; help protégés identify and remember strengths when they get discouraged; bring out protégés' best by challenging and encouraging them at the same time; be both role models and confidants; share mutual interests with protégés; and enjoy mutual acceptance and trust, which may often be the foundation of a lifelong friendship.
- The most successful protégés seem able to articulate dreams and goals, be passionate about pursuing those goals, work hard to achieve them, take the initiative to seek the help they need, make good use of that help, and recognize skills and talents of colleagues and collaborate with them.

There was much more, but the big-picture concept that emerged for Rich from these two years was a new model: dual mentoring strategies that he dubbed closed-system mentoring and open-system mentoring and detailed in his dissertation.[*]

---

[*] See appendix 3 for a full description of Richard Caruso's two mentoring systems developed at the London School of Economics and his third system used in creating his new company, Integra LifeSciences.

In Rich's memory, 1990 would become tagged as the year he earned his PhD. It was also the year that the horse farm in Chester Springs was suddenly sold. The horses were gone, but memories were left—including the Jeff Robbins story that Rich seemed to always find especially hilarious. It was about Miguel, one of the partnership's clients. He'd come from Panama for a yearling sale held in Kentucky, and he wanted to see the famous racehorse Secretariat, who was "at stud" on nearby Claiborne Farm. Jeff's tale was that he and Miguel "got to the farm, approached the fence, and saw the stallion at the top of a hill on the far side of the paddock. When his handler called him, Secretariat looked up, stared hard at us, then came charging down the hill right toward where we stood at the fence, and spit a huge mouthful of grass all over the front of Miguel's expensive, pleated, white, silk shirt! On Miguel's next visit, when I asked him if the grass stains had ever come out, he laughed and roared 'NO! I framed the shirt, grass stains and all; it's hanging in my living room!'"

As much as Rich relished the stories Jeff Robbins told, it's probably safe to say that Rich valued even more the nickname Jeff gave him that same year. When Jeff had moved to the farm to train horses, the farm's owner had promised him that he and his wife, Pat, and their twin daughters could always live there. Their daughters had cystic fibrosis, and the farm was where Pat staged her fierce battle for their lives. She grew all the family's food, so the girls grew up with "organic and local" as a given, not a slogan. Jeff and Pat built a house on the farm for her parents to live so they could be close and help out. In 1990, the girls were in their teens when the farm's owner announced abruptly that he was selling the farm and they had to leave—no discussion.

Rich felt the unfairness keenly. He helped them move and hired lawyers, suing the farm owner, winning, and forcing him to liquidate his company. Jeff and Pat were able to pay Rich back for all the attorneys' fees and remained grateful to him and Sally for the rest of their lives. Jeff said of Rich, "He's mild mannered, even shy, but when he gets angry at injustice, he's like the Incredible Hulk."

Rich could channel his anger to repair injustice and could use his very good brain to figure out some of the nuances of mentoring, but right then it was almost time to leave London and go home. Before leaving, though, he had a little mentoring of his own to do.

When he was still completing his dissertation in 1990, Rich had asked Fran's youngest child, Dana, to fly with him on one of his trips back to London. As she remembered it, "I'd just graduated from college, and he wanted to show me the city. I still have some pictures we took together in a photo booth at the airport there, which Uncle Rich thought was great fun. I also remember his sitting in a particular chair in his flat and writing out pages of his thesis by hand!"

Dana had early memories of her uncle sitting in another chair talking to Jerry and David and her in turn—assessing them, she'd felt then. Now with grown-up eyes, she saw a different Uncle Rich, doing school work too, just in his own way. She remembered when he used to take her and her brothers out for cokes. "He'd always get two large drinks instead of four small ones and divide the two big ones because it was less expensive that way." She saw that he was still both generous and frugal. She grinned, realizing, "I think he just looked for the deal and enjoyed that."

He showed her London's sights and showed her around the college too: "It turns out that the London School of Economics offered a one-year master's program, and I decided to stay for the year and get my master's. It was a wonderful year . . . opportunity . . . experience." Dana smiled, remembering. Rich could mentor and study mentoring at the same time, of course.

By the end of 1990, as Dana began her degree in London, Rich finished his and went home to what came next.

CHAPTER 7

FALLING SEVEN, RISING EIGHT

1990 TO 1996

All the money in the world cannot solve problems unless we work together. And if we work together, there is no problem in the world that can stop us, as we seek to develop people to their highest potential.
—EWING MARION KAUFFMAN

. . . and what came next would save lives.

Rich's goals included doing something that is "intellectually challenging," uses "leading-edge technology," "benefits all humanity," and "hasn't been done before." This project checked off all four of those goals—well, actually, along the way it met all nine.

His first twenty-plus years with LFC Rich had spent helping existing start-ups succeed. This time he'd start one himself—something medical. Baby boomers were getting older, so, he reasoned, were likely to bump up the need for health care, just as they'd increased sales of diapers, toys, schooling, and every other good their age cohort had needed. Also, Rich had noticed that medical research was coming up with all kinds of new products and treatments.

For the past two years, he'd been checking in every other weekend at the Radnor office with a small team that was researching ideas for the new venture. Now, PhD finished, he'd focus on this medical start-up for LFC.

The first successful heart transplant was in 1967, the year Rich began with LFC. Back then, using an organ from a dead person's body to replace a damaged organ in a living person's body had seemed just short of a miracle. When Rich read an article on the progress of organ transplantation in 1990, however, his thought was, "While organ transplants can certainly be successful and provide a chance for normal life, it seemed a rather primitive practice for our modern society."

Really? "Primitive?" His multidimensional mind came to that conclusion with a train of thought that went something like this:

a. The human body generates its own body parts at the beginning of life; shouldn't that ability still exist throughout life, even if slowed down?

b. Our bodies recreate new skin when it's cut, knit bones back together when they're broken. Surely, then, bodies can remake other parts; surely we can figure out how to foster, even reproduce, that process.

c. What we breathe-drink-eat, how we move-feel-think, all affect how genes turn on and off, how healthy bodies are. So as we learn more about how actions affect bodies, will we find that bodies can do more than we've thought?

The term *epigenetics* (how experience affects how our genes affect us) was coined the decade Rich was born but still rarely seen in the popular press of 1990. *Biomimicry* (using nature's strategies to solve human problems) had appeared in print less than a decade before Rich wrote his dissertation. So where did these thoughts of his come from? Had he been reading scientific articles, or had he come up with these ideas on his own?

Last—or maybe first—Rich learned from his own life: "I know that simple changes in my attitudes and actions have affected my own brain. Deliberately attending to the development of my brain has improved my functioning in all areas of life. That means to me that our bodies and brains are capable of miraculous change and growth, are adaptive and elastic, and that we probably aren't even close to learning *how* adaptive."

He'd come to believe that regenerating human body parts was possible. If the brain was so elastic, other organs and tissues could be too, he thought. With the right tools and knowledge, we could replicate what the body has already done once, could create a new body part when needed.

Some would call that belief audacious. To Rich, it seemed only logical, just science. He'd use his same old strategy of keeping on working until you solve the problem, so, of course, he "defined the primary objective of this start-up as *finding a way to have humans regenerate their own organs and tissues*." Rich's life and steady work had brought him more than he'd envisioned, so by this point in his life, embracing big visions seemed pretty sensible.

He understood that "the current consensus in the medical field at the time was that this type of technology was impossible to create." That was one more reason it seemed the perfect focus for Rich: "This effort sounded like a lofty goal to many people, but the fact that others had attempted it without success motivated me to pursue the idea even more enthusiastically." Solving problems was his fun—hard ones were just more fun.

Sally grinned telling a friend once that some people called Rich "a loose cannon"—as if that were a bad thing: "He was one of the few in his company who hadn't graduated from Princeton, but he was assigned all the hard cases because he could always turn things around. He was really good at solving difficult business problems. Whatever he did turned to gold." She'd learned to trust his business instincts.

They had homes not only in Villanova but in Greece, Florida, and Colorado too. They traveled, lived very comfortably, and—more than anyone else knew—helped others quietly, exactly the way both Rich and Sally liked it. By then, Sally had come to take their good fortune for granted, but her faith was based on more than the abundance and ease in their lives. Even though Rich could come across as a bit diffident in some social situations, in business, he had the confidence of someone relishing a well-played game.

He didn't bring work problems home. He didn't seem to have any, in fact. She knew he lost money sometimes, but he didn't appear to let it bother him. He thought of himself as "a conservative risk taker." His out-of-the-mainstream ideas were balanced by a big streak of frugality, a willingness to lose some money if necessary to explore a new idea, and clarity about just how much he could safely lose.

Sally's trust in Rich's business abilities, developed over a couple of decades, would soon turn out to be helpful—it was about to be tested.

In 1991, Dana completed her master's degree in economics and came back from London to work with Uncle Rich. She and others would turn his thesis on mentoring into a book, making his research more accessible to businesses, while Rich and his team would start a business. It would use both the closed and open versions of mentoring he'd researched but would especially embody the third kind he'd uncovered since getting home—collaborative mentoring: "After coming up with the model of collaborative-system mentoring, I wanted to put it into practice in this medical start-up at LFC. It seemed the perfect opportunity to do that because my knowledge of business wouldn't be enough this time. With no background in medicine, I'd need to work with persons whose strengths were completely different from mine. If we could move away from a rigid hierarchical corporate structure and combine the expertise we'd gained over time in our individual specialties, we'd get the best results from this hybrid we were about to create."

In Rich's mind, "there couldn't be one person exerting power-over strategies at the top, insisting, 'We have to do it this way to profit financially' or 'We have to do it that way to be safe medically.' We have to find a way that works from *both* perspectives, sharing power with each other and learning from each other as we grow. We have to learn to shift naturally and easily between the roles of protégé and mentor to get the best results from collaborating."

Rich and the group he'd coalesced were getting pretty comfortable with this kind of collaborating, when LFC pulled the plug. About a year after he came home from England to stay, Rich remembers, "The LFC executives' oil endeavor had become unprofitable, and the board decided to cancel both their oil venture and the medical start-up my team had been working on."

Right away Rich assembled the scientists and others with medical backgrounds who'd been advising him and made a verbal commitment to them that he'd find a way to continue the project. To keep that promise, he asked LFC's board to let him buy the medical company personally. In 1991, they agreed.

Before then, a pharmaceutical company named Marion Laboratories had bought from Harvard University and Massachusetts Institute of Technology (MIT) the right to make "artificial skin." Its inventors were John F. Burke, MD, an eminent surgeon-researcher at Harvard who specialized in treating burn victims, and Ioannis V. Yannas, PhD, a biological chemist working in mechanical engineering at MIT. Rich went to Boston to meet them both. He wanted to find out how they'd developed it.[*]

When Dr. Burke had worked in the burn unit of Massachusetts General Hospital, he'd realized that burn patients often died from dehydration or bacterial infection because so much of their skin, which keeps essential fluids in and foreign bodies out, was destroyed. To prevent these deaths, doctors tried grafting skin from unburned parts of the body onto the burned parts, when there was enough of the healthy skin left. If more than half of a patient's body had been burned, there usually wasn't enough.

Burke became determined to save more patients and began realizing he'd need help. In 1969, he asked Ioannis Yannas to share the work of finding a way for a large area of damaged skin to heal itself. Dr. Burke brought knowledge of biology, the structure of skin, and experience with burn patients. Professor Yannas brought understanding of DNA, chemistry, and plastics. They learned from each other, built on each other's contributions, and came to share a vision. It looked like *collaborative mentoring* to Rich.

Together they created a skin-like material by combining collagen and polymers: chain-like molecules that occur naturally—in spider silk, horn, and hair, for example—or can be made synthetically, as in some plastics. They tested this artificial skin matrix first by implanting it into animals. It provided scaffolding onto which the animals' bodies could regenerate new skin while at the same time protecting their bodies from infection and dehydration.

After success with animals, Burke and Yannas combined shark cartilage and cow tendons to make collagen that created a made-from-nature layer of tissue-like scaffolding. They then placed a synthetic layer of silicone on top of this artificial skin.

---

[*] See appendix 4 for the backstory on how Burke and Yannas created the first tissue-engineered skin and how Richard Caruso obtained the rights to it.

The silicone layer protected the damaged skin from bacteria and infections and kept the moisture in, while the collagen layer acted as a foundation on which they hoped new, healthy skin cells would grow on humans. Would they?

In one trial, and another, and then another, human bodies used that collagen-silicone structure to grow new skin and new blood vessels, bridging burned-out gaps between healthy skin. As the new skin grew, the shark cartilage and cowhide-tendon materials were degraded and absorbed: a little human composting going on.

When a scaffolding of this temporary artificial skin was implanted in a human body where skin was burned, that body grew new dermal tissue. It grew both the dermis and epidermis layers. It grew both in about eighteen days. Rich had to have felt in awe.

It was science. It was scientists' determination. It was meticulous work. It was visionary. To people it would keep alive, it might seem like a miracle. That's how millions had felt about a decade earlier when the whole world watched a man step onto the moon, but news of this miracle would spread more slowly.

First, it had to be approved by the US Food and Drug Administration (FDA), which had been established in 1906 to ensure the safety of foods and medicines sold to the public. It was supposed to make sure that nothing it approved would later turn out to be slowly killing people. "Buyer beware" had been consumers' motto for generations, each purchase in effect a personal experiment on oneself. Now FDA's seal of approval saved lives, but getting it took a while.

Two years earlier, Marion Laboratories had begun the process of proving to the FDA that their "artificial skin" was both effective and safe. As the back-and-forth dragged on, Dow Chemical bought Marion Laboratories and merged the company with Merrell Dow Pharmaceuticals.

The new owners let Marion Labs go through several rounds of applying to the FDA and being asked for more evidence. Then someone at Marion Merrell Dow decided that (1) this regeneration-of-dermal-tissue concept was too new, (2) the FDA would never approve "Integra Artificial Skin," as it was called, and (3) they'd sell Marion Labs' subsidiary, Colla-Tec, which made collagen for the artificial skin. They'd give up the license to make Integra skin—why bother? It wouldn't work anyway.

That's when Rich got involved. He felt excited. The project met his criteria. It was a risk that fit his dream of helping others in a big way, and he pursued his dreams. He also carefully checked out any risk before he took it. After learning from Dr. Burke and Professor Yannas how their artificial-skin technology worked, he called Fred Cahn, a PhD from MIT who was already working with Rich on the team to create another start-up. They carefully went over the ideas and technology involved: Were they missing something? What was the weak link? Could this really work, get to market, actually help people?

Fred saw the potential too. They'd try to buy the license. By then, though, that license was already back in the hands of Harvard-MIT, who told Rich they couldn't approve licensure of the artificial-skin technology to his group unless the inventors agreed. So Rich went back to Burke and Yannas. They agreed to license their invention to Rich's team. They also agreed to join the team as consultants. This was starting to look real.

Since they could get the license to make artificial skin, they'd need to get the equipment used for doing so. It was still owned by Marion Laboratories, so Rich made an appointment, took an early flight to Kansas City, and went directly to the front desk. There, he was told that Mr. Ewing Kauffman, now-retired founder of Marion Labs, had come in for the express purpose of meeting him. Rich had no idea why but, of course, said yes.

It turns out they were kindred spirits.

Kauffman walked in using a cane. He was in his midseventies then, a quarter-century older than Rich. A trophy in the large room recognized Kauffman as founder and former owner of the major-league baseball team the Kansas City Royals, so the older man and the younger man talked baseball for a while. Kauffman had started the team to grow a sense of community and pride in his beloved hometown—only one of many things he did to help others.

When he'd been about Rich's age, he'd started a foundation too, the Ewing Marion Kauffman Foundation. It, like UIF, was created to make positive change in the lives of others through support, instruction, encouragement. They didn't call it mentoring, but that's what they did. The same year Rich and John established UIF, Kauffman created a program he called "Project Choice," helping teens get through high school with good grades, no drug use, and what he called "good citizenship." If they met those three criteria, he paid their way through college or other schooling they qualified for.

He asked Rich about himself, and they soon learned how much they shared. Both men had humble beginnings, found the path of education, made more money than they'd known was possible, and figured out ways to use that bounty to help develop the huge potential both of them saw in human beings.

Then they talked about Marion Laboratories, this hugely successful pharmaceutical company Kauffman had started in 1950 out of his basement, selling homemade calcium supplements he made from crushed oyster shells. When he got ready to retire and sold the company, he'd counted on its continuing to develop the promising technology for making artificial skin, but soon Marion Merrell Dow gave up on that. Kauffman wanted Rich to know why.

In the past two years, Kauffman's health had pulled him away from active involvement in the artificial-skin project, and his perception was that its new managers hadn't been as optimistic, or as persistent, about it as he had been. He thought they'd given up on artificial skin much too early.

He wondered if they'd even understood the technology well enough to defend it to the FDA or make tweaks needed for improving it. There wasn't a regulated protocol for applying the artificial-skin scaffold on the operating table, no standardized instructions for using it. That meant doctors often didn't apply it properly, causing complications and increased pain for some patients, thus reducing the number of positive outcomes reported, which may have slowed FDA approval. Then there was another problem Kauffman saw: the new owners seemed to be reading motivations into FDA's reviewers, seeing their numerous follow-up questions and requests for additional data as a sign that the reviewers weren't convinced the technology could ever do what the data suggested, a sign that they were just slow-walking their ultimate rejection of the skin rather than acting out of honest concern about its safety and efficacy. Also, if FDA uncovered a weakness in the process, Marion Labs would have more work to do before getting approval. They had convinced themselves that FDA would never approve the product.

Ewing Kauffman wanted Rich to know that the problems with Integra skin could be solved, that it wasn't just a dollars decision, that all the extra time and work would be worth it in the long run because it would save so many lives. He wanted Rich to take a longer view; the money would come eventually. It was important to pursue this work.

What *did* Rich want to do with the artificial skin? Kauffman asked. He felt heartened when Rich explained that he'd use it to grow new skin for burn victims and hoped it could also play a part in regenerating other body parts for patients in need of transplants. Kauffman heard Rich's vision and determination. He saw mirrored in Rich his own persistence, problem-solving skills, and commitment to doing good.

They talked for three hours.

When they parted, Kauffman told Rich that he'd invest in this new company, but he may not have told Rich how relieved he felt: finally he'd found the person who'd manifest this dream he hadn't been able to make come true. He hadn't lost a long-distance race after all—it had turned out to be a relay, and now he could pass the baton.

Rich thanked Kauffman for sharing so much information and insight. He thanked Kauffman for being his mentor.

Several months later, in 1993, Rich read in a newspaper that Ewing Marion Kauffman had died. The foundation named after him lasted and grew, carrying on his work of helping others. On its website, there is a quote attributed to its farm-boy founder: "All the money in the world cannot solve problems unless we work together. And if we work together, there is no problem in the world that can stop us, as we seek to develop people to their highest potential." Rich couldn't have agreed more.

Just months before, in 1992, after more than twenty years with them, Rich had resigned from LFC to concentrate on the Integra project.

Making the artificial skin required not just the equipment Rich had bought in Kansas City but also the collagen made by Marion Laboratories' subsidiary, Colla-Tec. When Rich attended a presentation for potential buyers of the company, he met Judi O'Grady, the Colla-Tec employee who gave that talk. Rich's negotiations to buy it succeeded, and he asked Judi to be part of the new company.

She remembers being in Washington, DC, with him soon after: "We were at an attorney's office finalizing purchase of intellectual property related to the project, including all of Marion Labs' submissions to the FDA. Then we were going to the FDA to discuss next steps in getting those applications approved. As we left the attorney's office and were hailing a taxi, Richard turned to me and said, 'Congratulations! We now own Integra Artificial Skin, and when we get to the FDA, you'll oversee addressing the issues with getting FDA approval. You're in charge of Regulatory Affairs, and getting through their process is your primary goal.' He told me he was confident I was the right person to lead this effort and promised to bring this important technology to market. That was the real start of my career at Integra."

Rich supported and challenged Judi: "He was the most important mentor in my career." But then she grins and shares an example of what she calls "a little reverse mentoring" too: "One year, FDA scheduled a pivotal meeting for us at 9:00 a.m. on the Monday after Thanksgiving. Senior-level FDA reviewers of Integra Artificial Skin would meet with us for one hour to discuss how we could address their issues and possibly move toward obtaining their approval. Dr. John Burke and other physicians were attending, and so was our regulatory attorney. Richard wanted to attend too, but he also wanted to speak. The attorney advised that the FDA reviewers were most likely to get their questions answered if the physicians gave the message for Integra. He was concerned that Richard would take up our hour with a business message that wouldn't give FDA what it needed, so he recommended that Richard not give a presentation. When I told him this, he said, 'But Judi, I have to talk. I have to let FDA know how important this technology is.'"

Rich and Judi kept talking until they found a middle way. She helped him prepare a very short presentation and practiced it with him. Relieved, she reported later that "the meeting went well. Richard kept to the script."

He returned the favor not too long after. Judi met with FDA over more issues, but this time with a new division head who was reviewing the data for the first time. That meeting did *not* go well. On the plane home, Judi called Rich to brief him on the meeting, and he took it with an equanimity she came to appreciate. All he told her was, "Judi, I have complete faith that you will work this out with FDA. Let me know what your plan is. One meeting is not going to stop you."

He was right, of course. Judi called FDA as soon as she landed and arranged another meeting. Rich had given her exactly what she needed right then. His unwavering faith in Integra included faith in her, which helped her reconnect with belief in herself, so she could keep on keeping on. His ability to see strengths in others that they didn't always see in themselves was only one of the reasons she'd later call him "brilliant."

Judi also said—and others who worked with Rich would repeat—what became almost a mantra: "Richard never, ever gave up on his dreams." They'd been in the trenches with Rich and come to see this steadfastness as courage.

It won't surprise any parent that when Rich's son Jonathan was still in school, he described his father's tenacity with quite different words: "My sophomore year in college, I was working on homework for accounting class and having trouble figuring out a solution to one problem. My dad looked at it and said, 'Jonathan, the professor didn't give you enough information to solve this.' I went back to the professor the next day, and he said, 'Your dad's right,' and then gave me the information I needed. I was amazed that my dad picked up on that so fast!"

It was a turning point for Jonathan. As an adult, he described it as "an eye-opening experience. I'd rebelled against Dad in my younger days. I valued academic learning, liked accounting, and thought he valued street smarts more. Now I was learning that he not only liked accounting too but could even be a professor of accounting! Later I found that he was also amazing at analyzing businesses." Jonathan grew closer to Rich from then on, and as he kept on living his own life, he came to understand his father's better: "It took me a while longer to understand that he'd needed street smarts just to get to college. When he got there, he figured out that he was good at learning. His bull-headed nature probably came from growing up in a poor family. That must have been hard. He probably needed all that determination."

Jonathan's accounting problem turned out to be a kind of gift for Rich. In the years ahead, Rich would be given awards for business achievement. He would accept them with sincerely humble words, but he'd like the praise. There hadn't been much of it when he was growing up. Everyone was busy keeping the family functioning. Doing your part was expected, and Rich got that. He'd held his ego in check pretty well and figured out some deeper levels of meaning in life—he'd been all right without much praise. Still, we're all born with a basic need to be appreciated, so getting those awards would feel good. They wouldn't feel nearly as good, though, as shifting in his son's eyes from "street-smart" to "professor-level smart," from "bull-headed" to "determined."

Rich had held onto himself well enough to tolerate the hurt when his young sons' unconditional love inevitably turned into push-back as they tried to find their own way. A grown-up part of Rich knew they had to and knew he and Sally had given their boys the confidence to do the rebelling they needed to do. It was a normal part of parenting, but it hurt anyway. He'd cover that up with work, of course; but sensing some new appreciation, even respect, from his growing-up son was welcome. None of those future awards would compare—wouldn't come close. Even the bull-headed can use a little boost now and then—and the timing was excellent.

Although Rich had bought Colla-Tec "at a loss cost" and had minimized risk as well as he could, "during this early stage, our company was hurting financially because we had large start-up expenses and no authorization to sell the product. Rather than relying on the traditional source of private funding, from venture capitalists, we depended on medical companies for investment funding because they had a better understanding of the science underlying Integra skin: both the revolutionary idea supporting it as well as the need for it. They also had a working knowledge of the slow FDA approval process and were less likely to lose patience with the delays that caused."

Rich's retelling of that time sounded matter-of-fact. Others recalled it as a period of uncertainty, which reached Rich even at home. Peter, in his teen years then, felt it: "I remember Dad getting angry calls from people who had invested money in Integra Science when it wasn't doing well. I heard him trying to calm them down over the phone." About twenty years later, Peter quipped, "Today it's worth over three billion; I hope they kept their money in Integra!"

During those will-they/won't-they years for Integra, life around it kept right on moving. Rich's dissertation became a book titled *Mentoring and the Business Environment: Asset or Liability?* The Business Performance Group, a management research institute at the London School of Economics, had published it in 1992. Rich dedicated it to Sally, Jonathan, and Peter, and in it he thanked Dana for her help with the manuscript. One of his London professors, Keith Bradley, wrote the preface. It had the expected high praise but also included a few lines that gave a careful reader some clues about *why* all this mentoring mattered to Rich.

It said that "mentoring . . . is now viewed as a serious means of gaining competitive advantage," cited Rich's research showing that companies "benefit significantly from a *mentoring culture*," and added that Rich used "finance as a metaphor" to help businesses see the value of human beings to a company (i.e., that money's only a rough tool for measuring value, not the value itself). A bit of the inside Rich had slipped through all the business speak.

It was during those building-Integra years that Rich and Sally began making some additions and changes to their big old house. Around then, Jerry had met a master builder—of structures as well as of relationships—and started telling Uncle Rich that he ought to get this guy named Italo to work on his house instead of the contractor he'd already hired. It took a while for Rich to listen.

It didn't take him nearly as long to hire Bonnie. After she'd followed her uncle's example by getting her degree in accounting, she'd worked as a controller for a few different companies. In 1995, Provco had an opening for an accountant, and Rich called her. She still remembers that day: "He said he needed someone he could *trust*—imagine how great I felt! He had such a successful business, and he wanted me to do the accounting for him. I took the job and learned so much from him! I was married by then, but when calling people, I'd use my maiden name because the Caruso name was so respected. The only way they got me to leave was about five years later when I was pregnant with my twin boys and was put on bed rest. I was very upset about leaving Provco, but I knew they could manage without me."

The year Bonnie began at Provco, Integra was still seeking FDA approval and needed a significant investment to stay in business. It had to be from someone who could wait a while, and Joe Nichols turned out to be the key to that. He was a member of Integra's advisory board. Years before, he'd helped develop the collagen materials at Colla-Tec. Then he'd worked with someone at Johnson and Johnson who later became an executive at Boston Scientific, a young company that in the early 1990s needed collagen. That young executive contacted Colla-Tec, remembering Joe's connection with it, which is when Rich got involved: "I told them we wanted them to invest in Integra, and they did: $5 million. It was our first big investment." Indeed. That tided them over.

The moment when the big news came seemed to be stamped on Judi's brain: "Finally, seven years after we'd started the company, seven years of intense collaboration, seven years of an unbelievably arduous approval process, the FDA approved Integra Artificial Skin." It was right there on paper—in legalese for sure but still right there in black and white. Integra had kept claiming for all those years that it could trigger the human body into regrowing big patches of its own skin: an absurd proposition! Yet the paper said it was so. FDA agreed with them that their claim of "regenerating dermal tissue" was true!

Actually, it was a first for the FDA too. Integra's persistent insistence on making Burke and Ioannis's work helpful to the world had broken down a barrier of disbelief. Future applications for regenerative medical technology were likely to take not quite so long.

The group Rich had brought together to form Integra definitely knew how to work, how to collaborate, and how to persist, but they weren't all that skilled at celebrating. Judi was, though. At a local store, she bought an expensive bottle of Dom Perignon champagne and, back at Integra, she and Rich and the entire team toasted this improbable, audacious goal they had worked on for so long and kept believing in together when it seemed no one else did.

When asked about that time, nobody mentioned celebrating. What Rich talked about suggested how wholeheartedly he had assumed they would get that approval. He'd spent the time putting in place all the pieces they'd need to take the next step as soon as approval was given.

One of those pieces was Telios Pharmaceuticals, a public company that had spent $100 million developing another wound-care product but then gone bankrupt. Rich acquired it in August of 1995 and used its public status to raise money for Integra: "I took Integra public under the NASDAQ ticker name of IART and raised $30 million in the public market, which gave us the funds we needed to prepare our artificial skin for sale."

There'd be many other moving pieces to come: a radical's widow, some surprising recognition, a CEO with no experience in running a company, a big miscalculation, a change of strategy—but right then, finally, Integra LifeSciences Corporation was launched.

CHAPTER 8

REGENERATION

1996 TO 2015

*What I was doing made me so happy that there
was no need for financial compensation.*
—RICHARD E. CARUSO

Apparently the FDA *could* move fast at times. It gave Integra's artificial skin an award for Notable Breakthrough Device of 1996 soon after approving the skin as safe for use—after seven years of scrutiny.

Around then, Integra was audited, and the accountants found a glitch: Rich hadn't been taking a salary as president, which was "financially misleading," they said. He hadn't wanted a salary during those starting-up years, hadn't wanted to be reimbursed for footing the initial expenses either, because he wanted this business to be about his nine goals, mostly helping others—and he could get by fine without a salary anyway. He took it, though, for then, to keep the accounting in line with expected norms, so it didn't raise alarms.

Dana had stopped working for Uncle Rich in 1993 and in 1996 got her own award: a degree from George Mason University's School of Law. The following year, she gave Rich his only chance to be Father of the Bride. On December 13, 1997, he walked Dana down the aisle to marry Chris Conner.

It was 1997 too when a house fire badly burned Betty Shabazz, the widow of Malcolm X, and Integra's artificial skin was used in trying to save her life. It received much positive publicity then, even though in the end, the burns, on more than 80 percent of her body, were so severe that she died.

By 1998, more than 60 percent of the burn units in the US were using Integra's invention. It worked well and saved lives, but there was one problem Rich didn't know how to fix.

Calculations were that about ten thousand persons a year would need Integra's artificial skin and that most of them could now be saved by remaining hospitalized the several months it often took to heal. The problem was that few had the means, or enough health insurance, to cover such a long stay.

Public policy and the insurance industry could find a way to save those lives if they chose. Meanwhile, Rich, as president *and* CEO *and* chairman of the board for Integra, had to keep his company solvent. He became convinced that Integra couldn't thrive by selling *only* artificial skin: "It seemed that the best way to grow this new company would be to expand our product selection. If we acquired existing products, ones already approved by the FDA, we could get them to market sooner and keep Integra sustainable."

With his own vision and tenacity, Judi O'Grady's drive and skill, Joe Nichols's brilliance and serendipitous connections, plus their focused team, they'd gotten through seven difficult years; but they'd come close to going out of business while waiting for FDA approval. Rich would just as soon not go through that again.

He searched for new businesses Integra could buy while also working on Plan B: hiring a new CEO and president for this next stage. Rich looked at a few people with medical experience but wasn't sure any of them could run a company. Then he went back to someone he'd met over a year ago. Stuart Essig hadn't run a company either. He didn't even have a medical background. He did have a PhD in financial economics and an MBA. He was interested in medical technology and worked as a senior executive for Goldman Sachs in sales and acquisitions for their medical customers. He was on the partner track there and could have stayed, but he wanted a new challenge. He wanted to try running a company. Also, Rich had a feeling about him.

Actually, Stuart and Rich had talked about the possibility of Stuart running Integra months earlier, before it had gotten FDA approval. Stuart hadn't been interested in running a potential business, though—he'd prefer an actual one.

Still, he and Rich had kept talking. After FDA approval came through, they began talking specifics. Early on in their discussions, Stuart remembers, "I drafted a hundred-page agreement because I knew boards and founders can be incredibly hard to work with. As it turned out, I never picked up that agreement. Over the past year and a half as Rich and I had gotten to know each other, and as he'd introduced me to most of his team, we'd also built such a trusting relationship that all the if-thens in that agreement felt irrelevant."

By 1998, Stuart had become both CEO and president of Integra LifeSciences. Rich remained chairman of the board, which meant he wouldn't have to take a salary anymore but could still support Stuart. Wanting Integra to be about the goals was one reason Rich didn't want the salary, but he had another reason too: "What I was doing made me so happy that there was no need for financial compensation."

It had been clear to him since his first job at Price Waterhouse that the part of business he relished was the getting-it-started part, so this hand-over to Stuart didn't surprise anyone who knew Rich well.

David, in his thirties by then and working for Integra, may have encapsulated his uncle's decision best: "Public company CEO is not his style. As soon as a company becomes public with formal meetings, Uncle Rich isn't interested. He doesn't interact in that way. He has no problem giving up control to others after he's done what he wanted to do . . . and anyway, by then he's on his way to some new idea."

Stuart agreed: "When I became CEO of Integra, Rich stepped away from everyday business. He was a mentor and advisor, but he disengaged from daily decisions. If he had an idea, he'd tell me and say, 'Think about it,' but he didn't give directives, never undermined things I tried, was very supportive."

After hiring Stuart, Rich called to tell David, vacationing then, that when he got back to work, he'd have a new boss. David noticed things and people. He understood that Rich hadn't wanted David to be surprised when he returned, had wanted to be the first to explain the change to his nephew.

Also David understood why his uncle hadn't mentioned Stuart's joining the company until it happened: "He didn't want anyone to be disrupted by things that were still just ideas, didn't want anyone to worry about uncertainty."

David had gone into accounting, as his uncle had, and had taken to heart much of the advice Uncle Rich had given him during those growing-up years: "Try different things, read the *Wall Street Journal*, learn from your failures. Learn all you can about everything because learning helps you see life from new angles; all of it helps you be in charge of your own life."

He'd listened, but mainly David watched what Rich did: "Anyone could walk into his office. He treated everyone exactly the same: didn't treat 'important people' differently in any way from anyone else."

David also, and especially, noticed kindness: "A single mother of two who worked at Integra would occasionally leave work to pick up her children, run an errand, or get groceries. Rich had great empathy for others. Sometimes he'd notice her leave, ask if he could go with her . . . and then buy all the groceries for her family."

Then there was Jimmy—well, James DeJesus—who'd been hired by Joe Nichols years before and migrated to Integra with him. Jimmy had lost the use of his legs in an industrial accident. David noticed that just about every afternoon Jimmy would roll into Rich's office and Rich would lift him up out of his wheelchair—so Jimmy could feel again what it was like to stand up.

Eventually David learned the rest of that story. Jimmy had gotten a poor financial settlement after the accident. When Rich found out, he had the case renegotiated for a better deal, including a van Jimmy could drive by himself.

Things like that were what Rich meant when he'd written his fifth goal, to *personally* help make other people's dreams come true. The fourth was to benefit all humanity, and the eighth was to create opportunities for others. He'd achieved those last two goals, through Integra and other businesses, but that wasn't enough. He wanted the *personal* part too. He wanted to *know* the persons around him—wanted human connection in all parts of his life.

Building an addition to his Villanova house was no exception. Rich kept finding problems with some of the work done by the contractor he'd hired, and Jerry kept saying, "You need to get this guy who's worked on my house, Italo. He's really good."

Italo Manzi was twelve years old when he'd begun working in construction, at first in his native Italy and later in Switzerland. Following World War II, there were structures to be rebuilt all over Europe. As he'd worked on them, Italo had learned, and honed, the careful skills required, never needing a blueprint. In 1972, he'd brought all those skills to America. In 1999, Rich finally called him.

The first day Italo showed up at the Villanova house, he almost left when he met Chuck, the contractor, and Bill, his helper. Italo didn't want to take anyone's job. Did Rich have a contract with them? When Rich said that he'd hired them on a time-and-material basis, Italo agreed to try working *with* them for a few days. He'd see how that went.

It didn't go well at first. Chuck didn't like the idea at all and was less than welcoming to Italo, not realizing that this smiling Italian man had learned as much about people as he had about buildings. As he assisted with a few jobs, Italo began seeing errors Chuck and his helper had made in work they'd done so far. Instead of judging the men, though, in his quiet, unassuming way he helped: helped them fix some of the mistakes they'd made, helped them solve some of the problems they faced. Even as Italo redid some of the work they'd done, Chuck began realizing that Italo was actually trying to help him keep this job, not lose it. Soon, Chuck was coming to Italo, asking him how to do things.

Italo may not have ever heard the word *mentoring*, but living that cycle of giving-receiving-giving help seemed to permeate his life as thoroughly as it did Rich's. So did being frugal.

When much of the redwood Chuck had ordered for the addition was being tossed into a dumpster after mistakes had been made in measuring and cutting it, Italo unobtrusively asked Rich if they could keep those scraps to use later for things like doors and railings and edgings. Apparently, living life without wasting things was as much a value for him as it was for Rich.

In a completely different way and different layer of his life, Rich seemed to have met a man who was as fully his kindred spirit as Ewing Marion Kauffman had been.

After a certain phase of Rich's house addition was finished, and Chuck had learned some skills from working with Italo, and there was enough construction work in the area for Chuck to find other jobs, Rich let him go.

Italo stayed on, and as he stayed, his family grew. He'd married in 1971 and had three grown children by the time he began working with Rich. Before long, there were several grandchildren too, and Rich wasn't that far behind.

In May 2003, Rich and Sally watched Jonathan and his college girlfriend, Jennifer Bongard, graduate from Villanova University. Four weeks later, on June 14, 2003, they were married and then honeymooned in Bermuda. Jonathan had worked part time for his father during his senior year. After the honeymoon, he joined Provco Group full time. About three years later, in 2006, Rich and Sally became grandparents when Jonathan and Jennifer's first child, Kaitlyn, was born.

It was 2007 when Italo told Rich that he'd completed all the projects Rich had wanted done and that some other people were asking to hire him. Rich got very quiet then and didn't say anything for a while. Italo stood there, waiting. Finally, Rich said, "I don't think that's a good idea. If we get busy, you won't be there. Don't go anywhere—I'll have work for you." Then Rich asked Italo to be in charge of maintaining all his property and real estate holdings. Rich never asked Italo about money, never asked for plans or blueprints, and may have looked to admire but never felt the need to check Italo's work. They also shared a workman's pride in excellence. They'd come to trust each other.

Over the years, that trust extended to their families. The Manzis and the Carusos attended each other's children's marriages and grandchildren's christenings and confirmations. Sometimes Italo's wife, Phyllis, even made Rich his favorite Italian dishes.

One year, Rich gave Italo a copy he'd found of the 1921 *Architectural Digest* that featured photos of, and an article about, the Villanova house as it had been when it was first built all those decades ago—the house on which Italo had since done so much work. Rich and Sally had bought only four of the original twenty-five acres around their home. Rich laughed as he gave Italo the magazine and said, "If I'd known you then, I'd have bought the whole property!"

Most people who worked with Rich saw his friendship with Italo as just standard-Rich practice, knowing that his social life and business life overlapped. They also knew that many people draw a line between their business and personal worlds. That line may be set to ensure that there's no conflict of interest but may also suggest that the two require different value systems and ways of treating people: using power-over rather than power-with strategies, managing people as human assets rather than relating to them as human beings.

Rich didn't see it that way. He'd figured out the business world and operated well within it. He'd tried on parts of the culture of wealth—original art, big houses, luxurious travel—and he'd enjoyed all that. To him, people were just people, though, everywhere, with or without money. He knew about the watch-every-penny life. It just didn't seem to him that he was essentially different because he watched millions now instead of pennies. Besides, business was his fun, and he spent most of his time working on it. Where else would he make friends, and why not?

As soon as he became CEO of Integra, Stuart and his team began researching their now-proven "collagen-scaffold technology," which was successful in helping the body regenerate skin. Could it also be used to facilitate regrowth of other body tissue—nerves, tendons, gums, organs, even bone? In time, the answers were yes, and then yes again, and again.

DuraGen, for example, let the dura mater, the hard, outermost layer of the brain, regenerate itself after surgery. NeuroGen facilitated regeneration of peripheral nerves that had been severed.

It turns out they were pioneers in a new field in the medical industry. It was so revolutionary that there wasn't an official name for what they were doing—so they looked around. Rich remembered hearing a scientific speech given by someone who used the word *regenerative*, and he chose that. He liked *regenerative* vastly better than *artificial*, which wasn't accurate anyway; Integra had provided a scaffold over which the body could grow new, *real* skin.

Thus they branded their process *Regenerative Medicine*, and in time, the whole field was known by that name. When Rich wrote goal six, accomplish something important that hasn't been done before, did he have any idea it would be *this* important, *this* new? He may well have outdone himself this time.

In the first decade of the new century, more than a quarter of Integra's income came from this regenerative tissue technology that, it can fairly be said, *mentored* the body to regrow its damaged parts.

The rest of Integra's income came from dozens of other medical and surgical products made by the companies Stuart and his team kept buying. Integra was on its way to becoming the largest regenerative tissue technology and neurosurgery company in the world. Stuart's first foray into running a company had gone well.

If Rich's three-dimensional mind let him work on many things at a time, his strategies did too. His zest for start-ups, paired with his practice of hiring persons he'd known a while and come to trust, made it easy for him to hand over day-to-day control of businesses he'd created and to be glad for Stuart to put his own stamp on Integra.

In the same way, Rich had trusted John Crosby with the Uncommon Individual Foundation, right from its start in 1986. Since then, this foundation Rich loved had grown from John alone in a cubicle to more than a dozen full-time employees, a dozen-plus interns each semester and summer, mentoring programs in hundreds of organizations in the United States and globally, and thousands of persons experiencing the richness of a helping-each-other culture.

As that culture spread, more and more intentionally by then, Rich kept on living it as naturally as he breathed. He continued to mentor others, to be mentored by them, and to facilitate growth in various ways. One way he did so was as a board member—for Integra, of course, and for many others.

In 1996, for example, he'd become a founding shareholder of Interactive Investor International and had stayed on its board after it was sold in 1999.

Then there was Provco Group, founded in 1978, which had continued to provide funding and management for a variety of entrepreneurs with hundreds of millions of dollars in assets. Rich still served as its CEO and president when the first decade of the twenty-first century turned into the 20-teens.

Quaker Bio Ventures, a health care investment firm, was founded in 2002, and Rich began advising them soon thereafter, formally and informally, "in the spirit of mentoring," he said.

He advised venture-capital firms NewSpring Capital and ePlanet Ventures III; served on the boards of American Capital Mutual Funds and First Sterling Bank; and volunteered time on the boards of the Museum of the American Revolution and the Medici Archive Project, plus, of course, the Baum School of Art and Susquehanna University as well as the Business Performance Group of the London School of Economics.

He also served as chairman of the board of directors of Diasome Pharmaceuticals, a start-up founded in 2004 focusing on insulin-based therapies for treating diabetes; chairman of the board of CeeLite Technologies, LLC; CEO of Smart Personalized Medicine, a start-up LLC developing breast-cancer prognostic tests;

and on the board of Camel City Solar because he envisioned a way to revolutionize the solar power industry even before it became mainstream. There were many more.

Herb Brown, when introducing Rich to computers, had found that Rich could compute math problems faster than the computers then could. Similarly, when persons who handled day-to-day operations of companies shared their growing pains and next steps with Rich, they found that with his deep, wide experience, he could often cut through the details they were focused on, help them see the patterns involved, and guide them through the stages of growth he'd seen in so many other guises before. If they used his insights, they'd often succeed faster. It's no surprise he was sought as a board member.

It was around 2000 that the awards began. That was the year he was given the New Jersey Entrepreneurial Leadership Award in Biomaterial Science.

In 2001, he happened on some recognition that wasn't actually an award but may have felt just as good as one. As they had done on Friday nights in high school, sitting under the Ventnor pier, Rich and Ronnie Wagenhein got into a long conversation at their fortieth high school reunion. As Ronnie remembered it, "I was an IRS tax attorney and was telling Rich about a very complicated case I'd been working on. He got it right away, understood tax laws better than some tax attorneys I know—knew it like the back of his hand. He was also brilliant about the equipment-leasing field, and the size of transactions he was working on was amazing. He'd always been smart, but he must have just kept on getting smarter. I couldn't believe his grasp of finances!"

In 2006, Rich was given the Ernst & Young Greater Philadelphia Entrepreneur of the Year Award. Next, he and Sally traveled to Palm Springs, California, so he could receive Ernst & Young's Award in the Health Sciences first, and then the big one: its 2006

Entrepreneur of the Year Award for the United States of America, presented by Jay Leno, longtime television host of the well-known Tonight Show.

It was all pretty glamorous and exciting: good for Integra and fun for Rich. He took one quiet satisfaction from it that most people didn't know about, though. This annual Ernst & Young award had been endowed by Ewing Marion Kauffman, who'd spent millions trying to develop Integra's skin but soon before dying had sold the business to Rich. That's when Rich had told Kauffman that he'd make the skin a success, and he had. This award confirmed to Rich that he'd kept his word.

In 2007, Rich and Sally traveled to Monte Carlo for Ernst & Young's international awards, which attracted businesses from forty countries. That year, Cirque de Soleil won the international award for entrepreneurs. Rich's entry, combining Integra and UIF, came in second, but it garnered much interest.

By then, more than five thousand lives had been saved by Integra's skin alone, not counting any of its other products and even with no changes in availability of insurance in the US to cover its costs. By then too, UIF's skill in fostering mentoring cultures had saved thousands of careers and organizations from the stifling effects of too-rigid hierarchy. In his book printed in the UK, Rich had quoted one sentence from a senior staffer's evaluation of mentoring at his work, "Without the mentoring programme, the organizational structure of Motorola would fall back to rank-order bureaucracy." As UIF had spread the practice of mentoring, others had expressed similar opinions.

Sally teased Rich about all these awards. She was happy for him, glad he was being given credit for the good his vision and persistence had brought to so many lives. She'd been proud of him for a long time, though. She'd assumed that he was, justifiably, proud of himself too; but by then she could tell that, underneath the dignified acceptance speeches he was making, he felt deeply validated by all this recognition. It meant more to him than she'd thought it would. In fact, she was surprised.

She'd grown up with attention, warmth, support: "What a good job you did on that. Congratulations, Sally!" or "Of course you can do that. Would you like some help to get started?" Rich's family had loved him just as much, but there hadn't been time for all that. Besides, verbal affirmation just wasn't their style. He'd known they loved him. What he hadn't known was how good some of that praise could feel.

In 2008, he was given the Mid-Atlantic Capital Alliance Award in Philadelphia. In 2009, Drexel University gave him an honorary PhD in medical engineering, and he was asked to speak to the Entrepreneurial Summit at Bucknell. (Apparently someone had noticed what good use Rich had made of the master's degree he'd earned there in 1966.)

In that talk, he at first admitted to thinking of entrepreneurs as persons who took foolish or excessive risks, so he couldn't possibly have been one, saying, "I've always believed I was a very conservative risk-taker." Then he shared a bit of introspection: "Ultimately I realized that the more passionate I was about an idea, the better able I was to convince myself that the risks were fewer and safer than they actually were."

Those comments came in the early making-jokes, warming-up-the-audience part of his talk and so could be taken lightly. Or they could be seen as insight into his own mind, part of his "emotional intelligence," as it had come to be termed.

Rich went on in that speech to give the standard definition of *entrepreneur* as someone who "undertakes an enterprise," which in America, he said, means mostly business enterprises—but then he begged to differ. His expansive mind saw entrepreneurs as persons who "develop their entrepreneurial spirit and apply that spirit to whatever they find meaningful: education, research, art, business, government—anything." In that moment, Rich opened a peephole into who he was, sharing with anyone really listening exactly why he'd been able to help create a new field in medicine, to redefine that old word *mentor* and nudge it into the mainstream, and to have fun working hard at both.

Also in 2009, Rich made sure to attend the ceremony at which Abilene Christian University presented a Distinguished Alumni Citation to John Crosby. When Rich spoke at the recognition dinner that evening, he called the award "significant" and John's work "outstanding." For more than twenty years by then, Rich had known John's valuable achievements and fully trusted his wide range of abilities. He was glad that others had noticed too.

In 2011, Bob Pittello died. Several years before, Rich had gotten a call from his old football coach turned friend. Pittello had moved from mentoring young athletes at Susquehanna University to helping his hometown, Mount Carmel, in New Jersey. The morning he called, he'd lost a large investor in a town-improvement project and needed an immediate replacement. Rich, of course, did more than invest. He and Pittello worked together to bring Reinhart Food Service to the town's SEEDCO Industrial Park, providing over a thousand new jobs, enriching the community, and encouraging residents to stay in the area.

Rich spoke at Coach Pittello's memorial service, telling everyone there what a far-reaching difference in his life this old friend's support and encouragement had made. Another old friend, Bill Muir, was there too, and the college roommates got to reminisce.

Later, Rich and Sally established the Richard E. and Sally F. Caruso Mentoring and Innovation Center at their alma mater. The center was for mentoring students to pursue their own dreams. It was given in honor of Coach Bob Pittello and Coach Jim Garrett, both of whom had so effectively mentored Rich.

By 2013, Stuart Essig and his team had been growing Integra for more than fifteen years, adding on average four companies in each of those years. By 2017, it would grow to approximately 4,400 employees in fifty locations worldwide and would be selling thousands upon thousands of medical devices in over 130 countries. Financial reports would list Integra's gross revenue as $1.2 billion, with a market capitalization of $5.3 billion. That would be nice for the company's investors—especially Rich and a few others who had held on through the early lean years. Integra's international reach was gratifying too for all those doctors who could then save more lives. Integra's success even came pretty close to achieving Rich's fourth goal: "something that benefits all humanity."

Perhaps it goes without saying that early on, Stuart had had Judi O'Grady develop a mentoring program for new biotech hires. Soon Integra was receiving close to a hundred applications for each of the two-year positions. Most applicants had master's degrees already. Those accepted, called "associates," had four assigned mentors as they rotated through Integra's divisions. Afterward, they usually applied to work in one of those divisions, giving Integra an easy way to stay fully staffed with the best of its associates. Before long, other companies were asking how to start a similar program.

As Integra grew, Stuart followed Rich's example: delegating, building his bench, enriching the team. They hired Peter Arduini as president in 2010 and then asked him to take on the CEO position in 2012 when Stuart became chairman of the board, with Rich staying on the executive board of directors.

It was 2013 too when Rich began writing down his memories. Maybe that was another way to mentor. Could things he'd learned help others? Were there high school students planning to leave school in order to make money now who might read about Rich's life and catch a bigger vision for their own lives?

Sometime in 2014, Rich mentioned to John that he was having trouble remembering as well as he usually did. He'd read somewhere that meditating fostered mental clarity, so Kathleen Crenny stepped in. She did accounting for Provco, worked in the office next to Rich's, and found Pamela Urbas to come to the office once a week to teach various kinds of yoga and meditation to both of them. Kathleen practiced with Rich on the other weekdays. Over time, they used primarily a version of meditation called Kirtan Kriya because it seemed to help Rich most, and over time, at home and at the office, his meditation community grew to sometimes include Jonathan, Jerry, granddaughter Kaitlyn, and others. Occasionally, Kathleen and Rich went to UIF's offices, where John, staff, and interns meditated with them.

Later still, someone found Robbie MacLean, who introduced Rich to craniosacral therapy. That helped Rich relax. All of it helped . . . some.

By 2015, John had to accept that it wasn't helping enough. Another award came, and working with Rich on his acceptance speech was a different experience than ever before, for a couple of reasons.

First, the award came from the National Italian American Foundation—the NIAF Special Achievement Award in Business and Health. Everyone who knew Rich long came to understand how proud he was of his Italian heritage, so this one was personal. Rich always wanted his speeches to be written carefully, but he wanted to deliver them so they sounded spontaneous: no boring reading from a script for him, especially this time.

Second, the move from reading to speaking naturally was taking much longer. He was allotted three minutes to thank NIAF for the award, but remembering big swaths of the first three-minute draft wasn't going well. The second version was simplified to one minute. The third version was thirty seconds. He practiced this stripped-down version with John over and over with occasional success. Then he and Sally, with the contingency from Integra, Provco, and UIF, all in their gala dresses or tuxes, went to Washington, DC, for the big night.

John recalled, "My palms were sweating. Sally was tense. We were all tense as Rich walked to the podium to accept his award. As he stood at the mic and began to speak, I held my breath until he'd finished every word. That's when I took another breath, and that's when all of us clapped—maybe a little too hard. He'd nailed it!"

It was a bittersweet moment. Rich continued to receive awards, but none like this. This was the perfect one. Cono would have been so proud. As he'd gotten older and mellowed a bit, Cono had begun to brag about Rich's accomplishments to his friends and to Rich's. Maybe if he'd been in Washington that night, he'd have even been able to say out loud to his son how proud of him he was.

CHAPTER 9

CODA

Nobody is perfect.... Nobody is thoroughly bad either....
But we should try to further the good in ourselves and others.
—JAWAHARLAL NEHRU

For his sophomore year of college, Rich had lived off-campus in an apartment above a shoe store, which was next to a restaurant and bar. One of his roommates, John Pignatore, grinned remembering that, despite such easy access, "I never saw Rich smoke or drink alcohol. We teased him, saying he was 'incorruptible,' and he'd always deadpan back, 'Oh, you just haven't made me the right offer!'"

It's funny: by the final third of his life, Rich had helped so many people that most stories about him turned into accolades. Hearing them, you'd think he was some kind of saint! Part of his earnest charm was that he knew better.

He knew the part of himself that had skipped school and stolen hubcaps, lied about his age to buy beer for his friends, messed up his freshman year in college, missed his sons' confirmations, sometimes had his head filled with business doings when his family was right there in front of him wanting to connect. He knew he'd lost his own and some other people's money in a few deals. (Never mind that he'd made vastly more for others; it bugged him that anything he'd done had hurt anyone.) He knew all that, and more.

In fact, knowing and accepting all the pieces of himself, facing squarely the good and the not-so-good he'd done, was one of his strengths. Mostly his good-enough upbringing, plus his very good brain, had helped him conclude that he was made of pretty good stuff *and* had given him the sense to know that he had to work to develop that stuff. Seeing both his own essence ("I'm OK as is") and his own potential ("I have much to learn"), he could see good in other people too and also see where they had growing to do. That balance served him well.

Everyone who talked about Rich spoke of how he treated others and how well he could tell who would, or would not, fit a specific job. Peter Tyrell, Rich's friend from middle school in Margate, put it concisely: "Rich said that in business, 'It's not the deal; it's the people you deal with.' His uncanny ability to read people may have been honed by years of experience, but it seemed intuitive. He'd tell me not to trust a certain person, and he'd be right. His insight was uncommon."

Watching people began early on for Rich. Of course, all children watch the grown-ups they depend on: look for patterns, figure out what they need to do to feel safe. Still, Rich may have paid attention to people more closely than most. At least he certainly seemed to think more about what he saw and to wonder about results: How did that behavior work for that person? He thought about his own actions too, had a lot of ideas, and wanted to see if they'd work. Along with all that thinking, he noticed everything.

The results of all that noticing, watching, and wondering seemed to show up in his life in at least four ways. One was in his steady *hard work*, which it may have been impossible not to notice in his parents' lives. A second was in his *initiative*, starting what often seemed to others impossible. Perhaps that came from noticing, and taking advantage of, all the freedom he had within the reasonable structure of his childhood: When he had an idea, why not try it? No one was stopping him. A third was in his *persistence*, keeping on far beyond the point where others quit. Maybe that came from not being judged when some of his ventures failed or from noticing that he survived those early failures intact. What became a fourth constant in Rich's life was *helping others*: Did that come from noticing what others did for him, from noticing that whenever he'd done as much as he could on his own, somehow, from somewhere, he got the help he needed to take a next step?

Because of these characteristics, his high school coach John Boyd praised his exceptional football skills, paving the way to a scholarship from Coaches Jim Garrett and Bob Pittello at Susquehanna University. It was Garrett who coached him in football, mentored him personally, and wrote a compelling letter of support to his parents when he was suspended from school. It was assistant coach Pittello who inspired him to major in accounting, which served him well throughout his life. Ironically, if Rich hadn't messed up his freshman year, he would never have met Russell Baum, who came into his life at just the right time because, first, he noticed Rich's great promise. Baum stayed to mentor because he saw how receptive Rich was to learning and then saw Rich applying his learning to his life.

"Taking responsibility for one's own life," as Rich put it, was a thread throughout everything he did. For him, it seemed to be about the freedom to help himself and the wisdom to accept help from others. In turn, he mentored persons who wanted to learn and grow. A Provco employee, Michael Cooley, wrote to Rich one Christmas: "No words can express my gratitude. You have been an incredible inspiration and mentor. . . . Thank you for providing an opportunity and career I could only dream of." Such notes, words, actions, and thoughts of gratitude permeated Rich's life by then. They were welcome, and reinforcing, but not necessary. He helped people because "we humans are built to help each other" was a simple truth deep within him, and he lived his truth.

When the twentieth century was beginning, Louise Pirolli and Cono Caruso had left their birthplaces in Italy and moved to America. By the time the twenty-first century began, their thoroughly American family had expanded to four living children, ten grandchildren, and a slew of great-grandchildren.

Carmen, Fran, Rich, and Joe had grappled with whatever came across their paths and had created comfortable lives. Rich's life had become especially comfortable. He was even in danger of exemplifying America's rags-to-riches stereotype, but, of course, the richness of his life was much more nuanced than that—he didn't fit into any boxes. For one thing, he'd never defined "success" as dollars. It had been about making a difference, but in *his* way; helping people with ideas *he* dreamed up; giving rein to his *own* creativity; and doing what felt right to *him*. It wasn't *about* him, though. Thankfully, what usually felt right to him was long-term thinking about the greatest good for all concerned, so most of the financial success he'd created lasted.

Forty years after it had begun, the Provco Group, led by Jerry Holtz and Gary DiLella, was still thriving by helping entrepreneurs start sustainable businesses, investing in publicly traded companies, and acquiring desirable real estate sites for third-party tenants.

Thirty years old and counting, UIF was helping and investing in a different way. It had brought mentoring to many types of organizations that often spread the word about what they'd learned so that other organizations caught the bug. It had taught mentoring skills in classroom settings to more than twenty thousand youth and adults who then often mentored others, infecting them too. It had enlarged the definition of mentoring. It had also, arguably, helped infiltrate American consciousness so thoroughly that mentoring, a word seldom used in the twentieth century, had become ubiquitous as part of mainstream culture in the twenty-first.

John Crosby, with directors Joe Lopez and Michael Hackman, was still involved in running UIF. With staffers and interns, they managed outreach programs for vastly different groups: start-up entrepreneurs, corporations, businesses, colleges and universities, and schools. Their work touched persons barely participating in America's prosperity and persons dominating it. The foundation had fulfilled dreams and given hope to every age group. It had enriched organizations of all sorts by making them encouraging spheres of collaboration where people with their own visions could breathe and belong; could give their best and have it received; and, yes, could be financially successful—all other criteria being fulfilled in their lives, as Rich's ninth goal required.

After twenty years, Integra kept right on thriving too. Rich had seen the potential in new research when others hadn't and, with his team, had become a pioneer in a new field. He treasured his friendships with Stuart Essig, Judi O'Grady, and Joe Nichols. They had mentored, learned from, and grown to trust each other. Their strong relationships were a clear, if unquantifiable, factor in why Integra had become more successful than anyone had dreamed.

All of it had brought Rich both financial and soul-building rewards. These entities he'd nurtured were staffed with many persons whom he'd picked, mentored, or encouraged, including family and near-family: Jerry Holtz acting as CEO and Gary DiLella as CFO; son Jonathan working with Italo Manzi to maintain physical facilities and grounds; son Peter helping with investment research from home; and David Holtz working at Provco.

As Rich was having to pull away from serving on boards and advising companies and nonprofits, the organizations he'd helped create kept on doing what he'd set them up to do. He had done his work well.

Rich had consistently given away chunks of his financial success through the years: some known and tax-deducted, of course, and some private that others didn't know about. It took a little longer for him to pull away from that long habit too. Fran teased him about one donation he had made regularly. Rich had written, "I sent a contribution to St. Michael's School, the elementary school I attended in Atlantic City. It was enough for them to put on a fundraiser that let them keep the school open. My 7th-grade teacher, Sister Jeannette, was in charge when they received my first donation, and she called to thank me. I've sent her money for several years since." "Yes," Fran laughed. "He kept sending donations for years after Sister Jeannette had passed away!" Eventually the school closed when the character of the neighborhood changed so much that there weren't enough children to fill the classrooms . . . and eventually Rich got the word.

One thread that ran throughout Rich's life was family. He began life within it and was completing his life within it: at home with Sally certainly, and at work, which for Rich was another version of family. He'd used his dad's shoeshine materials to start his first business. A few years later when Rich had needed more income than one summer job provided, his brother Joe would staff a newspaper stand until Rich took over after working for hours as a waiter. Then in 1993, Joe and Rich collaborated on a skating rink at the Jersey shore in Egg Harbor, where Joe's daughter Kristin loved to skate. Fran's daughter, Dana, worked for Uncle Rich in Provco before leaving to go to law school. Carmen had invested with Rich in Rustler Steak Houses. Carmen's daughter, Bonnie, followed her uncle's example and majored in accounting. Later she went to work at Provco because Uncle Rich told her he needed someone he could trust.

In other words, for Rich, having family work for him was a huge plus. He didn't worry about "favoritism" because he trusted himself to hold accountable each person he worked with. Rich trusted himself to find each person's particular strengths and help that person find a way to use those strengths. Rich held onto family and mentored them just as they mentored him.

He held onto friends as well, describing them as "close friends and mentors, all of whom fill both roles."

When he worked with people and came to trust them, he'd try to keep them working with or near or for him as long as it fit for them. He'd seen Jim Sullivan's integrity and good sense when they'd worked together back in the Rustler Steak House days and later got Jim to serve on Integra's board.

Rich once remarked that with Stuart Essig, Judi O'Grady, and others at Integra, he had "a high-functioning relationship." Judi agreed: "Richard was an irreplaceable mentor to Stuart and the executive team. He was the greatest mentor I had in my career. He mirrored the definition of mentor and was the force behind Integra's success." In fact, the high-functioning relationships and company seemed to mirror each other.

When Rich began working with Italo Manzi and discovered what a gifted craftsman he was, he dubbed Italo "a master of all trades." Later he dubbed Italo a "friend" as well and hired him full time to maintain the companies' substantial real estate holdings as well as Rich and Sally's own home in Villanova.

Other partners left the horseracing business with a profit. Rich and Sally left it with profit too but also cherishing the lifelong friendship they'd forged with Jeff and Pat Robbins.

Working together was only one of the strategies Rich used for holding onto good friends. When his 7th-grade classmate Peter Tyrrell was seventy-four, he still described their relationship as "best friends." Maybe that was because Rich had picked up a phone and called Peter now and then ever since their days in Margate. Rich did the work of staying connected. He valued friends who knew all aspects of him, not just the "successful businessman" part. David Aiken, from whom Rich had discovered the fun of playing football, was another school friend Rich held onto throughout their lives. Before his death, David, an attorney, asked Rich to manage his estate. David knew plenty of lawyers with the skills needed, but he trusted Rich—so had Russell Baum, so had Bob Pittello, and so had many, many others. He trusted them back and lived safely within that trust after he learned that he could no longer trust the vast, rich networks of his own brain.

At first, Rich drove himself to work every day as usual and still solved problems when he got there—all those people he'd held onto and held close would catch any mistakes his rusting brain made. Eventually, Jerry showed up each morning to drive him to Provco, which had been Rich's daytime home for years. He'd still sit at his desk, and Kathleen kept coming up with ways to help him stay busy. One strategy she used was supplying him with find-the-words puzzles, which he worked hard at and always seemed able to solve. Once John sat down with Rich to help him figure out an especially hard one, but Rich figured it out first. Kathleen was a CPA, but soon John gave her a new title: "Best Caregiver Ever."

Rich kept right on doing what he could, as they all did. They helped him, kept him safe, and learned from him, just different things now: how much more patient they could be; how giving with no prospect of return feels; how fragile we all are; how "it takes a village" at both ends of life and so we'd better all stay close. Relationships matter.

Without thinking of it in those terms, Rich had created, as John would say, "a mentor-rich community." It was made up of family, extended family, and friends who were now work family. He'd mentored and learned from people all his life. He'd seen people as human beings who mattered. That is, he'd known no one was perfect because he knew he wasn't, and he'd known there was good that could be developed in everyone because he knew that part of himself.

Oh, he'd known he couldn't bring out the good in every single person, despite his best efforts. He hadn't kept close to everyone he knew—in spite of his keen eye for others' abilities, he'd had to let a few people go from work, had to fire them. Even then, though, he'd tried not to label them, to speak or even think of them as all bad. Maybe someday they'd get to work on the parts of themselves that didn't serve them well—it didn't have to happen now, with him.

That whole mentoring piece had always been key, though. If any of us had any chance of becoming the potential best selves inside us, we had to help and accept help from each other. That's one thing Rich had known for sure and done his best to imbue in everyone whose life he'd touched.

Whenever people spoke of Rich, they'd struggle with what felt like contradictions: he was school-smart and street-smart, generous and frugal, earnest and funny, "incorruptible" and "looking for the right offer." He knew to "stay away from that guy," but he'd never give up entirely on others—there was some potential to be developed there somewhere. He would take risks on investments no one else would touch, but he'd invest only what he knew he could lose. He coached both sons' baseball teams and did what he could to give them more attention than his own dad had given him, but he'd go to school in England for two years and see them only once every two weeks. He'd take them on wonderful vacations, but his mind would keep wandering back to work. Everyone who talked about Rich did this back-and-forth, ping-pong think-ing. Maybe we're just used to a black-white, good-bad worldview and don't have the words to describe a perfectly imperfect human being with highly developed strengths and more to learn.

As Rich's brain began failing him, he began going to Mass more often at his beloved Saint Katharine of Siena in Wayne. He would talk to the priests and church members more than he ever had. Perhaps it was a clue about how vulnerable he was feeling. Dementia was one of the few things in his life that his rock-hard grit couldn't fix.

Perhaps one of his failed business attempts exemplified Rich better than any words could. In the mid-1980s, still with LFC, Rich had spent months putting together two deals. In one, he negotiated the purchase of a $167-million leasing company owned by Electronic Data Systems and later sold it when General Motors bought the computer firm for a price that boosted LFC's accu-mulated assets to $750 million: about $749 million more than the $1 million LFC had when he'd joined in 1969. He'd earned his keep over those years.

In the second deal, he'd spent months working to buy bank-rupt Phoenix Steel, attending close to one hundred meetings to put together a debt-repayment schedule and convince its biggest creditors not to liquidate the company, which would cost more than a thousand Phoenix employees their jobs. Rich and his LFC partner Frank Slattery were buying Phoenix to keep it alive and save jobs.

After all those meetings and accepting Rich's offer, though, Phoenix Steel's board of directors turned around and accepted a buyout by another company that offered a higher bid up front, adopting the same repayment package Rich had put together. The court awarded LFC $300,000, although Rich said his cost was well over $1 million. Rich said the amount awarded by the court "doesn't even cover expenses."

Rich and Frank had lost a lot of time and money. Rich responded to that loss by giving away a little bit more. He gave about $120,000 to those employees whose jobs he hadn't been able to save, around $100 for each hourly worker, foreman, and office worker. Top management was excluded.

"My goal is the company's survival," he'd said. "That matters more to me than making money. The people who've really suffered in this bankruptcy process aren't the management or the customers but the employees."

It wasn't a lot of money—not enough to save most of the employees from personal bankruptcy if they couldn't find a job soon, and not enough for Rich to notice. He'd be fine financially, but he wouldn't be fine if he didn't somehow act on what he believed. Maybe this token gesture would at least tell the workers he saw them. He knew they were gutsy, had their own power. Most of them would make it, somehow, but they weren't invisible. They mattered.

When word had gotten out about Rich's gift, there'd been appreciation from the employees but suspicion from some not used to distinguishing "legal" from "fair," lulled by the "It's just business" mantra. "Is he doing it for a tax write-off?" they asked. "Giving away money with no gain? What's going on?"

"Anytime you show some compassion for your fellow human beings, you may be viewed as some kind of crackpot, and that's unfortunate," Rich had replied, feeling hurt, mad, sad, amused. He saw us all in the same boat, all just people.

Cono could have been one of those employees. Without the help he got, Rich might have been too. He didn't want to lose that part of himself. It was just as real and important as the has-lots-of-money part. He'd kept noticing all the parts of himself, kept them working together, and kept growing. He'd done his best to stay whole.

The nineteenth-century author Robert Louis Stevenson had written, "To know what you prefer, instead of humbly saying Amen to what the world tells you you ought to prefer, is to have kept your soul alive." Maybe that's another way to explain the kind of good man Rich had become and the good that he had done: he'd kept his soul alive.

AFTERWORD

UIF TODAY

2015 AND BEYOND

Those who seek mentoring will rule the great expanse under heaven.
—SHU CHUNG, *CHINESE BOOK OF HISTORY*,
CIRCA SIXTH CENTURY BCE

I n 1986, the Uncommon Individual Foundation, under John Crosby's leadership, began implementing structured mentoring programs in more than two hundred organizations and providing mentoring to thousands of individuals throughout the country and globally. The foundation's initial mission as written by John and Richard Caruso was "to work with people who are the most imaginative and creative in all fields and to encourage them to develop themselves to their fullest potential."

In 2014, the mission was expanded: "To educate, encourage and enable individuals to recognize the power of mentoring and its role in achieving personal success, inspiring change, and making a positive contribution to society."

Although the words *mentor* and *mentoring* were rarely used or seen in print in the mid-1980s, after six months of research and collaboration, John and Richard made the decision that UIF would become the first private nonprofit foundation devoted exclusively to mentoring. John began collecting research, writing curricula, designing mentoring programs, personally training mentors and mentees, and evaluating the mentoring process in different types of organizations.

Today, the foundation has grown exponentially to five major programs that incorporate Dr. Caruso's three models of closed-system, open-system, and collaborative-system mentoring:

1. Corporate (Structured) Mentoring Program

2. Entrepreneur Mentoring Program

3. Education Mentoring Program

   a. OnTrack to Post-Secondary Education Program

   b. Youth Literacy Mentoring Program

4. Technology Mentoring Program

5. Media Mentoring Program

1. CORPORATE (STRUCTURED) MENTORING PROGRAM

When the Uncommon Individual Foundation was created, John Crosby began studying the small amount of material available on mentoring in an open cubicle near Richard Caruso's office at LFC on the fourth floor of Radnor Corporate Center in Radnor, Pennsylvania. Twenty-eight years later, in 2014, UIF made its fifth move, this time to a four-story building in Devon, Pennsylvania. It used the first floor of 6,500 square feet to accommodate fifteen full-time employees; fifteen to twenty entrepreneurs; and, each fall, spring, and summer, approximately eighteen paid college and high school interns who were assigned to collaborate with entrepreneurs and staff in the expanded five programs.

Today, the corporate mentoring programs, originally called individually structured programs, continue to be designed and facilitated by Dr. Crosby. These planned programs have been provided to many organizations in the United States, including Fortune 500 companies such as Dow Chemical, IBM, Motorola, DuPont, and Eli Lilly; as well as businesses; state and federal government agencies; faith-based organizations; colleges; universities; public and private schools; youth organizations; professional associations; social service agencies; and entrepreneurial start-ups. UIF also has provided mentoring initiatives in the United Kingdom, South Africa, Sweden, South America, and other countries.

During these three decades, John and his staff have trained 20,500 mentors and mentees in intimate classroom settings and have received more than $1,250,000 in donations from organizations for planning and running these structurally designed programs.[*]

Praise for the Corporate Mentoring Program

Between 2000 and 2019, the foundation has provided thirty-six year-long mentoring programs in six divisions of the State of Delaware—nineteen consecutive years! Approximately 40 percent of both mentees and mentors in these programs have been promoted to higher-level positions, with an employment retention rate of 96 percent.

Barbara McCaffery said this upon receiving the distinguished Uncommon Individual Award in 2014:

---

[*] See appendix 2, "Ten Steps for Establishing a Corporate (Structured) Mentoring Program."

Barbara McCaffery, Mentor/Mentee

I am so grateful to work in an environment where directors will allow staff to participate in these programs. It has fostered in me so many creative ideas and has given me confidence not only to suggest them but also to initiate them. One thing I've noticed in other divisions that have been trying to get a mentoring program off the ground is that if it's not supported at the top, it will not happen. It can take just one person to open the door or slam it shut. I've been lucky to always work for people who fling the door wide open. Since I've been running the program for years, I now have plenty of data to support its success. What a leap of faith my director took! When I was developing the program, I had no data—just a gut feeling. Mentoring fosters a feeling of wanting to give back. That's why we get so many people wanting to stay involved in mentoring. It's loyalty that's hard to find these days.

Michelle Potter, Mentoring Program Coordinator

Dr. Caruso, I admire your success and your passion to help people worldwide. Dr. Crosby, I compliment your team members: Shari Sauer, Jessica Stokes, and Ben Pietrzk. I have worked with them for one year, and they are exceptional. With their guidance, I have learned so much about mentoring and have gained valuable experience. They are always professional and respectful yet personable. Together, they are a goldmine of knowledge and resources. The mentoring planning sessions, which have included program evaluations and problem solving, have been spectacular due to the wealth of their creativity. Everyone on your team is responsible and detail-oriented, which allows deadlines to be met promptly and the quality of the work to be superior. Your team represents your vision with the utmost passion and sincerity. I thank you for the opportunity to work with such a devoted team.

Monique Summers, Mentee

As mentees, we typically think of a mentor or mentorship as what someone can do for us: "What's in it for me?" Coincidentally, the key word in *Mentee* is *Me*. How can I make the most of this? I took the opportunity to see if my mentor could help me help myself. That may be hard for mentors who are super excited to make an impact and do something for their mentee. Deloris Hayes-Arrington must have secretly known I needed to be pushed—not by her but by myself.

After we met to go over my goals, she gave me another assignment, which was exactly the remedy to what I had been seeking as a mentee. I didn't know what to do next in my career. I had hit the glass ceiling in my unit, and I wasn't sure if I should break through the glass, climb over the glass, or just walk away. She asked a simple question: "What is your ideal job?" It sparked the flame that allowed me to blaze a new trail in my career.

I am blessed to have received your guidance, advice, encouragement and support, Doloris. You were an excellent example of what a mentor should be, and I pray for your continued success as a leader and motivator. A special thanks to Dr. Crosby, Christine Heard, and his team for their training I am grateful to have been among this group of successful "Uncommon Individuals."

Deloris Hayes-Arrington, Mentor

I was taken aback when Monique Summers so adeptly turned the table and used her newfound skills on me as her "test pilot" to develop her coaching capabilities. Who is mentoring whom here? I don't think I have had that happen before, but I really enjoyed it. Watching her blossom, expand, and grow was a mentor's dream come true. I do believe she exceeded her own expectations. She certainly exceeded mine. What a year! What began as a traditional mentor-mentee relationship soon evolved into a dear friendship of confiding and going through the highs and lows of life. We have decided to continue this friendship since we enjoy each other's company. I cannot wait to see what the next years bring for Monique. I only know it will be exciting and rewarding.

Sarae Black Hayes, Mentee

There were so many intriguing classes offered: Mentor-Mentee Training, Effective Communication, Personality Types, Grammar in the Workplace, How to Ace an Interview, How to Score on an Application. But the one I enjoyed the most was Public Speaking. Each participant was asked to choose a topic to train a group of "aliens" new to planet Earth on things we "earthlings" were familiar with. I trained the aliens on washing windows.

I introduced myself as a professional window washer of my own company, "Doing Glass with Class." I was shocked to learn how many people enjoyed my pseudotraining. At that time, my mentor encouraged me to take a serious look at making this a career choice.

During the program, Dr. Crosby constructed a self-assessment tool designed to highlight the career areas we would most excel in based on an extensive survey. That assessment matched 92 percent of what my mentor noticed that day.

I am so thankful for this program and my mentor, Jill McCoy. Yesterday I was a tech, today an office manager, and tomorrow a trainer. In the future, I intend to give back as a mentor myself.

Principal, School District of Philadelphia

I would like to express thanks to the UIF for the presentation to the mentors involved in the Philadelphia Elementary Principal Intern Program. Your well-prepared presentation was enthusiastically received by our mentor principals. Your knowledge of mentoring and ability to interrelate mentoring with our particular program was outstanding. I appreciate the support of the foundation in providing assistance to the School District of Philadelphia and look forward to an ongoing relationship.

Vice President of Training and Mentoring, Denver Seminary

Thank you, Dr. Crosby, for your invaluable contribution to our First National Conference on Mentoring. Your plenary address and workshops were well received. Many spoke of the excitement and energy of the many participants. Thanks for being such a great cheerleader for mentoring in theological education and for your personal words of encouragement.

Superintendent, Oak Ridge School District, Oak Ridge, Tennessee

Thank you so much for the inspiring training workshops this week. I've been a giver and a taker of workshops for twenty years, and so I can be especially critical of both delivery style and content. You had a wonderful, calm, credible tone throughout, even with our potentially challenging audience. You listened and responded so graciously in incorporating people's ideas, suggestions, and challenges. I enjoyed the listening-to-you parts, the reading-of-the-book parts, the working-in-pairs-and-small-groups parts—a wonderful balance of participant techniques.

2. ENTREPRENEUR MENTORING PROGRAM

Upon receiving Ernst & Young's 2006 Entrepreneur of the Year Award in the United States, Richard Caruso began talking with John about expanding structured mentoring to help individuals in their start-ups by creating UIF's Entrepreneur Mentoring Program (EMP).

EMP collaborates with UIF-vetted entrepreneurs as they bring their products or services to the marketplace from concept to commercialization. The program assigns two to three paid student interns to each chosen entrepreneur to assist in the business development process—writing business plans, identifying their client base, analyzing the marketplace, designing websites, and refining and testing product/service concepts. These high-performing students from local colleges, universities, and high schools have the title of entrepreneur associate or entrepreneur associate assistant. They come from diverse backgrounds and are enrolled in various degree programs at colleges such as the University of Pennsylvania, Villanova, Temple, Penn State, Swarthmore, Eastern, La Salle, Saint Joseph's, Rider, Susquehanna, Bucknell, Hamilton, Washington and Lee, and the University of Delaware. Some attend high schools such as Philadelphia's Central High School, Julia R. Masterman, Conestoga, Haverford, Hill Top, West Chester, and Upper Dublin.

Entrepreneurs who participate in EMP develop their organizational talent and expertise, explore new market opportunities, and create pathways to investment. Joseph Lopez, managing director, and Ben Pietrzyk, assistant director, together with the assigned entrepreneur associate interns, help these creative individuals consider their business model from every possible angle, teach them to evaluate and manage risks effectively, and plan for future growth as their ideas come to fruition. Entrepreneurs enrolled in the program actively engage with a network of other entrepreneurs and mentors from industry, government, and higher education sectors that provide professional advice. The current roster of participants is active in the field of education, health care, communications, health and wellness, and medical devices.

In addition to business development, participants can hotel office space at the foundation to host meetings and conduct their day-to-day work. Access to physical space is another endowed service of the foundation designed to create a "mentoring community" for individuals who want to learn more about entrepreneurship.

A key goal of EMP is to propagate the concept of "Entre-preneurial Philanthropy"—the contribution of expertise, skill, and knowledge to advance other entrepreneurial pursuits. As entrepreneurs receive mentoring benefits through UIF, they are asked to engage in Entrepreneurial Philanthropy by giving back to the foundation. Unlike other business incubator programs that charge fees or require an equity stake to participate, UIF expects entrepreneurs to give back one hour of mentoring time for every three hours provided by the associate interns and staff. Entre-preneurs can present at UIF events and workshops, support fel-low entrepreneurs, mentor high school and college interns as they explore interests and career options, volunteer their time and expertise at partner schools, and advocate for the foundation.

Since 2014, EMP has helped entrepreneurs raise $1.4 million in capital while creating more than eighty jobs. In the process, UIF-affiliated entrepreneurs have received more than one hundred thousand direct mentoring hours through the program and saved more than $3 million in business development costs.

Praise for the Entrepreneur Mentoring Program

Participating Entrepreneurs

Ellen Hamilton, ChemoCozy

I became affiliated with EMP very shortly after I launched my company, ChemoCozy. I believe I was one of the first participants, and I know I had the longest run. The program provided not only support via a variety of resources but also a warm, encourag-ing environment that was most helpful to me when faced with challenges. EMP grew structurally during my tenure and because of that, my company is now starting to experience the growth

I was hoping for. Additionally, EMP interns were an invaluable resource. I am so thankful to have had the opportunity to work with some tremendous young people who took my product and mission very seriously, resulting in them being instrumental to my sales growth!

Diena Seeger, iBalans

iBalans is the developer of a transformational mindful philosophy for harmonious, youthful movement. Based on the principles of neuromuscular science, iBalans develops sensory-stimulating training products for mind-body fitness and rehabilitation. We are so grateful to Dr. Caruso and the foundation for all the project support and guidance and for fostering collaboration with other participating companies (thank you, ChemoCozy!). It's been such a huge help to have our extended team sharing our enthusiasm for serving our clients and looking ahead for ways we can build momentum. The diversity and depth of support particularly from Chris DiAntonio, Michael Hackman, and Lucy Lopez have enabled us to achieve our goals within our budget.

Nic Freschi, Solar Divide

UIF was absolutely essential in helping me and my cofounder get started with our first start-up. The staff there is unbelievably supportive—especially Joe Lopez and Ben Pietrzyk, who always took the time not only to offer constructive criticism but also to put their own energy into doing whatever my cofounder and I needed to get our company off the ground, including connecting us with investors who ended up offering us $50,000 in seed funding. The foundation also worked with our team to refine and perfect our pitch, which was indispensable in Solar Divide ultimately winning the $30,000 grand prize of our college's business plan competition. Because of UIF, we ended up with $80,000 in funding, pro bono legal services, and lifelong mentors and friends while having fun the entire time.

College and High School Associate Interns

Mary Catherine Jones, Bucknell University

Gratitude is another common word that can sum up my summer entrepreneur associate intern experience. I am so grateful for the vision of Dr. Caruso and Dr. Crosby. Their passion and commitment to the foundation are evident every day in the work being done at 80 West Lancaster Avenue in Devon. I consider myself very fortunate to have the privilege to say I worked at UIF this summer. The experiences and learning moments I have had here are truly priceless. It is a rarity when you can look forward to going to work each day and count the tangible learning experiences you encounter each day. I could never say thank you enough! (Mary Catherine became a senior associate the following summer.)

Cassidy Brown, Hamilton College

This summer, I had the amazing opportunity of being an entrepreneur associate for UIF. The experience not only provided me with a strong skill set to progress in the working world but also fostered strong mentoring relationships and a community of growth, individuality, and drive. I worked with five entrepreneurs and saw the business side of creating an app, getting investors, conducting market research, experimenting with Squarespace, and so much more. One-on-one interactions with entrepreneurs allowed me to cultivate knowledge in an assortment of business areas. The UIF staff and affiliated entrepreneurs truly care and value the young associates working with them.

Monica Clark, Rider University

The entrepreneur associate program has helped me learn and experience many real-world situations that you cannot get by sitting in a classroom learning about business. It has given me many new skills as well as strengthened old ones that I believe will help me be able to succeed in the real world after graduation.

Sravya Basvapatri, West Chester East High School

Through this program, I've gained real-world experience working with those in fields in which I am interested—entrepreneurship and business management. As a rising high school senior, being able to find this experience has been invaluable and extremely helpful to me in understanding the different projects and considerations that go into launching and running start-ups within far-ranging fields. In addition, working within the amazing environment and culture at UIF, where everyone is willing to teach, learn, and share advice, I have advanced my skills, both socially and professionally.

3. EDUCATION MENTORING PROGRAM

In the fall of 2012, under the direction of an experienced guidance counselor, UIF created a new college and career readiness e-learning platform called OnTrack to Post-Secondary Education. OnTrack became the foundation's first education-specific program tailored after Dr. Caruso's deep belief that educational attainment is an essential ingredient in achieving personal success.

Under the leadership of managing director Michael Hackman, the OnTrack team accelerated the e-learning curriculum to include a classroom-based format called the OnTrack Workshop Series. Then in 2016, the foundation launched a Youth Literacy Program designed to address the literacy gap among K–5 students who do not read at grade level. Both of these programs are based on a blended learning model, combining an e-learning curriculum with hands-on supervision, counseling, and mentoring.

a. OnTrack to Post-Secondary Education Program

UIF's OnTrack to Post-Secondary Education Program is an online e-learning system designed to empower 9th- through 12th-grade students with the knowledge and skills to successfully graduate from high school, understand their options to achieve and fund a postsecondary education, and realize the value of mentoring in their lives.

OnTrack is delivered through short, grade-specific videos that increase a student's knowledge and confidence level about getting into college or other post-secondary programs. The curriculum is carefully vetted by a national panel of guidance counselors and delivered through a series of approximately two hundred five- to eight-minute videos. The two hundred topics include navigating high school, career and college planning, financial aid, financial literacy, study skills, and social/emotional learning. This web-based program provides high-school-age students, school counselors, teachers, parents, mentors, and community organizations with a step-by-step guide to the college process.

In alignment with the foundation's "strength through mentoring" philosophy, OnTrack students are able to invite a parent, guardian, or other interested person to be their mentor through the OnTrack experience. The program links students and mentors with the tools they need to maximize the student's goal of getting into the college or another postsecondary institution of their choice with adequate funding in place.

Under the leadership of Andrew Zivic, director of college readiness programs, OnTrack has helped more than five thousand students better understand the process of achieving and funding a college, technical school, or other postsecondary education.

In 2016, with the successful experience of OnTrack, Michael Hackman launched the OnTrack Workshop Series taught by Shakia Kirksey, assistant director of college readiness, as a supplement to the e-learning experience. In-person workshops provide more in-depth content to the online learning. By meeting the needs of every individual student, the foundation is working to make the postsecondary application and adjustment process as simple and stress-free as possible.

Praise for the OnTrack to Post-Secondary Education Program

12th-Grade Student

I absolutely *love* OnTrack! I feel so much better about researching colleges and things like financial aid, scholarships, campus life, and so much more! I have gotten rid of a lot of my anxiety about college thanks to OnTrack!

11th-Grade Student

The OnTrack videos are so helpful. I never dreaded completing assignments for this class; I honestly looked forward to watching the videos. They gave me so much information, I always watched more than one. In this program, I learned that there are tons of ways to prepare yourself for college. I have also learned ways I can stay organized and on top of things. The people in the videos give links for you to use to study for the SAT/ACT, research different colleges, and so much more. I would recommend this to any student looking to go to college. It's a great program!

11th-Grade Student

I love OnTrack. I feel that this website is very helpful to students in all grades, and it helps the students be on board with their work and feel secure that they will be able to afford to go to college and be able to continue an education for themselves as they prepare for the real world. I feel that OnTrack has definitely helped me more with my study skills to achieve better success while in school.

Public High School Teacher

OnTrack is a great program to use. It helps cover topics we may not be able to get to during the academic year. The students like being able to complete modules from their phone, and they love that it's computer-based.

Upward Bound Program Coordinator

OnTrack provides a systematic way for us to ensure that our students receive appropriately timed and paced and high-quality content regarding academic and social skills as well as college access and readiness information. It is an excellent complement to the mission and daily work of our curriculum.

Educational Talent Search Program Coordinator

OnTrack is an additional resource for students. This program leads to more in-depth explorations on careers and getting ready for college. It blends well with other programs we use for college and career research.

Upward Bound Program Coordinator

OnTrack provides a systematic way for us to ensure that our students receive appropriately timed, paced, and high-quality content regarding academic and social skills as well as college access and readiness information. It is an excellent complement to the mission and daily work of our curriculum.

b. Youth Literacy Mentoring Program

In the fall of 2016, the foundation launched a new program targeted at improving the literacy levels in elementary school–age children. Under the program director, Betsy Dwyer, UIF works with schools and youth-serving organizations to provide literacy-based partnerships, program management, and funding. The model is partnership-centric, bringing together schools, youth development organizations, e-learning providers, and funders to achieve the goal of improving literacy levels of disadvantaged youth. The program provides additional literacy support to the students to enable them to attain on-grade-level reading skills. Additionally, the Youth Literacy Mentoring (YLM) program is designed to pair high school and college students with elementary students to provide coaching and mentoring around the importance of learning to read. The mentors share their love of reading with the younger students.

These programs operate during after-school time and as part of a summer youth camp experience. Students move through three thirty-minute rotations of small-group literacy instruction, iReady computer-based education modules, and homework support.

Praise for the Youth Literacy Mentoring Program

Student, 5th Grade, E. M. Stanton School, Philadelphia
iReady helped me because I didn't get a good grade in reading during the school year. It helped me by giving me stories to read, and I liked answering the questions too. I don't think I would've gotten this much help if I stayed home during the summer.

Student, 4th Grade, E. M. Stanton School, Philadelphia

I liked the program because it helped me learn words I didn't know before. I liked working with the teacher. It was like having my own private tutor.

Brad Steese, Program Coordinator,
Charles A. Melton Center, West Chester, Pennsylvania

The iReady software, along with the additional support offered by the UIF teachers, has allowed us to give our after-school-program students a chance to advance their reading and literacy skills during the academic year. Our summer camp uses iReady to keep students engaged in reading and literacy so they don't fall behind over the school break. The support, data, and other teaching tools offered by iReady and UIF have become true assets in our youth academic programs. We have seen major improvements in less than a year!

Parent of Peyton, 3rd Grade,
Laura Waring Elementary School, Philadelphia

Peyton didn't like to read much before he began attending the summer program. In the course of two and a half weeks, he is coming home and picking up books and reading them to himself and to his little brother.

Parent of Trevon, 1st Grade,
Laura Waring Elementary School, Philadelphia

Well, when he first started the program, he couldn't really read books, but now he's bringing the books home and is able to read. Being that we have ten kids, it helps us as a family too.

4. TECHNOLOGY MENTORING PROGRAM

UIF's Technology Mentoring Program (TMP) places trained staff and volunteer mentors in elementary and middle schools in the Greater Philadelphia Area to facilitate STEM workshops for students and enable teachers to augment their current curricula in science, technology, engineering, and mathematics.

The program, directed by Chris DiAntonio with Jon Rodriguez and Almondo Santos and tech associates (college juniors/seniors and recent graduates), provides mentoring support to schools and community organizations to enhance their existing resources and provide staffing knowledge to implement STEM programs. The goal is to generate interest and raise awareness about STEM careers while allowing children an opportunity to gain hands-on experience with coding, robotics, virtual reality, video game development, drone technology, 3-D modeling, and 3-D printing.

The tech program can be customized for any particular audience from introductory single sessions to year-long engagements, both in class and after school. The foundation offers technology mentoring at no cost to students or education partners. By bringing technology and mentors into the classroom, TMP provides new, engaging, and meaningful project-based learning to students.

TMP began in the spring of 2016 with a single 3-D printing presentation at Richard Caruso's parish, St. Katharine of Siena, located in Wayne, Pennsylvania. Less than two years later, TMP has expanded its programming to seventeen schools and community-based organizations in Philadelphia and surrounding suburbs, providing more than two hundred STEM presentations and 670 in-class mentoring hours. In total, the program had reached one thousand students by the end of the 2017–18 academic school year.

Praise for the Tech Mentoring Program

Student, 8th Grade, St. Martin de Porres School

Overall, this program has been a great experience for me. It really broadens your perspective of current technologies that are becoming more noted in this electronic generation. My mentor-teachers not only taught and demonstrated 3-D printing but also taught programming, virtual reality, and drones. I have learned so much these past two years in being in this amazing program. It truly has been a unique experience.

Student, 8th Grade, Ss. Colman-John Neumann School

Seeing these presentations showed me many new and innovative ways to learn and perform daily tasks. I really do believe it is the future of our lives.

Christina Elisio, Tech Teacher, St. Katharine of Siena School

St. Katharine of Siena School has been beyond blessed to have been given the opportunity to work with UIF that was established by Richard Caruso. He and Dr. Crosby have taken mentorship programs to new heights that are touching the lives of teachers and students every day. Our students are full of excitement when they get to create different technology-based projects with the UIF teacher-mentors. We look forward to working together for many more years with the foundation.

Richard Ollinger, President, Cornerstone Christian Academy

UIF has become a major player in helping Cornerstone Christian Academy shape and advance its technology program for students. In collaboration with school administrators and teachers, UIF mentors have helped launch the very popular "Tech Titans" after-school computer club for middle school students. This weekly project-based program gives interested students an opportunity to engage in STEM education beyond the classroom.

Michael Marrone, President, Liguori Academy

Our partnership with the Uncommon Individual Foundation has enabled our students to realize the many possibilities and opportunities that exist in the technology world. The partnership in the Tech Mentoring Program has given students hope and much to look forward to as they move in the right direction of life. We are so blessed with the opportunity to work with UIF.

Meghan Baskerville, Technology Teacher,
Ss. Colman-John Neumann School

TMP has given our students an opportunity to explore cutting-edge technology concepts. These concepts presented by the mentor-instructors include computer programming, 3-D printing, virtual reality, and a hands-on demonstration of drones. The mentors are knowledgeable and give our students a chance to learn and explore technology concepts that will be used in the future.

5. MEDIA MENTORING PROGRAM

Communication has changed dramatically since 1986, and UIF continues to evolve to meet the demands of the twenty-first-century media culture. According to a 2016 study by eMarketer, the average American spends more than four hours on mobile devices every day. In today's digital world, videos make up a majority of online content. It was only natural to launch a Media Mentoring Program (MMP) in 2016 to provide training in communication, branding, and video production to individuals and organizations engaged with the foundation. Through in-person and video-based mentoring, MMP helps entrepreneurs, students, and working professionals define and deliver marketing messages to reach intended audiences.

Under the leadership of former journalist and media professional director Lucy Lopez and program coordinator Jacob Smolinski, the media program has created hundreds of videos and two successful web series and launched a state-of-the-art multimedia studio called UIF REC Studio.

Lucy and Jake, together with their college interns, have dramatically increased the recognition of the foundation, its mission, and mentoring services across the Greater Philadelphia Area and in social media.

Richard Caruso Mentoring Series

The Richard Caruso Mentoring Series is one of the many programs produced to exemplify the life experiences of Dr. Caruso.

From humble beginnings as a boy shining shoes in Atlantic City to jump-starting multiple businesses (including FedEx, CNN, PECO, Verizon, and Integra LifeSciences—which saves lives by regenerating skin for burn victims), Richard Caruso embodied the American Dream.

While achieving success in business and garnering many accolades along the way, Richard never forgot the mentors who inspired and motivated him. As a result, UIF established the Richard Caruso Mentoring Series, which profiles how the power of mentoring helped other leaders overcome setbacks, realize success, and become the entrepreneurs of their own lives.

From tenacity and innovation to leadership and managing risk, the broadcast-quality video series provides real insight into the lives of innovators in business, medicine, education, and the nonprofit sector.

UIF REC Studio

In the fall of 2018, the foundation launched REC Studio, a play on Dr. Caruso's name—**R**ichard **E**. **C**aruso—which is located in downtown Wayne, Pennsylvania. The goal of the multimedia studio is to produce hyperlocal video content centered on the theme of mentoring. The studio features the people and businesses making a difference in and around the Greater Philadelphia Area and uses their stories as tacit mentoring resources to guide and inspire others.

ON/UP Philadelphia

ON/UP Philadelphia is a documentary series dedicated to the stories behind entrepreneurs and the mentors that help them succeed. This series is made possible by UIF and showcased across social media platforms.

   ON/UP is shining a light on the people of Philadelphia making a difference in industries, communities, and everyday lives in the City of Brotherly Love.

The Richard E. and Sally F. Caruso Mentoring and Innovation Center, Susquehanna University

On Saturday, October 6, 2018, Susquehanna University dedicated the Richard E. and Sally F. Caruso Mentoring and Innovation Center with Sally cutting the orange and maroon ribbon in the Blough-Weis Library. The endowment made by Richard and Sally to their alma mater serves as a dedicated collaborative learning and mentoring space at the heart of the campus. In addition to the space, the Caruso family's gift will enable the school to fund a yearly "Innovation Competition" and prize through the business school and provide funding to support the school's Center for Economics, Business, and Entrepreneurship Education. This fund is in honor of James W. Garrett and Robert Pittello, Richard's football coaches at Susquehanna from 1961 to 1965, whom he credits with instilling in him the values of hard work, preparation, persistence, and pursuing his dreams. He honors them for teaching him how to develop a value system, work in a team environment, and develop, focus, and realize those dreams.

Praise for the Media Mentoring Program

Entrepreneurs

Joe Burdo, Cofounder, CFO of NeuroTinker

During the fall of 2017, NeuroTinker ran a successful Kickstarter campaign to crowdfund the first manufacturing effort of our science education products. The media team was indispensable in helping us plan, script, and execute our video. Without them, the success of our Kickstarter campaign would have been much more uncertain. I can't speak highly enough of our time with the media team—it was fun and resulted in a great finished product.

Sgt. Major Marty Kenny, The Weekly Fight

In May of 2018, *ON/UP Philadelphia* featured Sgt. Major Marty Kenny of The Weekly Fight, a nonprofit that transforms posttraumatic stress disorder into posttraumatic growth. The videos reached nearly six thousand people across social media within the first few months.

Sgt. Major Kenny wrote about the experience: The media team from start to finish was a pleasure to work with. It was much less of a "shoot" than it was a conversation about The Weekly Fight. Their patience during the interviews can only be compared to that of a loving parent with their children. There was never an indication of frustration or exasperation on any of their faces. During our work-out, their interaction and video shooting went unnoticed. They were never in the way and were able to capture some intimate shots without making our members feel uncomfortable.

To have a product like this put out by this team for our group is very humbling. Their dedication and patience has made a major impact on our small nonprofit and we do hope that they recognize the impact they had on our community. I constantly tell people around us that we would not be where we are and growing where we are without the UIF team. The people in the media team from UIF have without a doubt played a role in our success.

THE FUTURE

UIF continues to innovate in the field of mentoring. The leadership and staff are always searching for new applications that create a space for enterprising individuals to cultivate a rich, personal mentoring environment that helps them discover and release the uncommon individual within themselves.

The foundation's newest enterprise centers on the deployment of mentors in schools and community organizations. These Mentors-in-Residence (MIR) will be full-time, dedicated young professionals helping students achieve scholastic goals, pursue interests that benefit them personally or professionally, and develop skills that expand their career-choice options.

MIRs will be an additional, local resource to support teachers, staff, and administrators as they educate youth in socially and economically challenged communities. Leveraging UIF's core programs, MIR can work with teachers to mentor students individually or in small groups around specialized subject matter that has "real world" application for the student.

A few years ago, Richard Caruso said, "It is my privilege to collaborate with like-minded and stimulating individuals who want to take charge of their own lives and develop themselves to their fullest potential through our mentorship programs. Helping others create, implement, and sustain a vision of their own dreams continues to be a rewarding enterprise for me."

RICHARD CARUSO'S
NINE GOALS

1. Do something intellectually challenging.

2. Work with leading-edge technology.

3. Work with people I like and respect and who respect me.

4. Work on something that benefits all humanity.

5. Personally help make other people's dreams come true.

6. Accomplish something important that hasn't been done before.

7. Create a vision that others can understand and follow.

8. Create interesting career opportunities for others.

9. If all the criteria above are fulfilled, be financially successful.

TEN STEPS FOR ESTABLISHING A CORPORATE (STRUCTURED) MENTORING PROGRAM

T here is no ideal profile for planning a structured corporate mentoring program. However, based on more than thirty years of research and field experience, UIF offers the following step-by-step blueprint for designing and customizing mentoring programs in a variety of settings—corporations, businesses, government agencies, colleges and universities, public and private schools, faith-based organizations, youth groups, and other organizations. Using these steps as a generic guide, mentoring programs can be tailored to produce maximum satisfaction for mentors, mentees, and organizations.

STEP 1: Hold a planning session with UIF and key organization representatives to identify issues, goals, and desired outcomes and discuss how mentoring can help achieve these results.

STEP 2: Form a mentoring steering committee of six to nine individuals who reflect the diversity of the organization and setting.

STEP 3: Identify and appoint a coordinator who will be an active, on-site leader and liaison with UIF, get monthly feedback from mentors and mentees on how each pair is doing, and is highly committed to the success of the program.

STEP 4: Plan, publicize, and schedule orientation meetings to recruit and identify prospective mentors and mentees.

STEP 5: Match mentors and mentees using profile information about mutual goals, interests, and hobbies. Since multiple mentoring provides an added dimension to one-on-one matching, encourage mentees to engage other mentors and use a variety of resources (e.g., books, articles, lectures, quotes).

STEP 6: Help mentors and mentees clarify their goals and expectations through UIF's two core training workshops that teach specific mentoring skills they need to know to succeed in their respective roles.

STEP 7: Offer UIF specialty training sessions throughout the year that address specific mentor, mentee, and organizational needs, such as cross-gender, cross-racial, cross-cultural, and cross-generational mentoring; long-distance mentoring; managing change; facilitative communication; and team mentoring.

STEP 8: Plan small focus group sessions with UIF trainer-consultants so that mentors and mentees separately can get together, raise issues, listen to problems, ask questions, and get answers. Schedule a series of special events to remind participants that they are supported by the organization.

STEP 9: Distribute UIF's "Mentoring: How Are You Doing?" SurveyMonkey questionnaire periodically to mentors and mentees to gauge the level of activity in and satisfaction with the mentoring program. Feedback and written reports will be shared with participants as appropriate.

STEP 10: At the end of the established period (usually nine to twelve months), evaluate the success of the mentoring program in reaching stated goals and prepare a written report that summarizes findings. The evaluation should record, both statistically and anecdotally, reactions, successes, needs, and suggestions for changes that can be made in future programs.

John C. Crosby, EdD

RICHARD CARUSO'S THREE SYSTEMS OF MENTORING

CLOSED-SYSTEM MENTORING

Closed-system mentoring is a more precise definition of what Richard had been calling "structured" or sometimes "formal" mentoring: assigning a single mentor to help a sole protégé, to the exclusion of other mentors and resources. The mentor is considered the authority figure, the dominant influence, and the protégé benefits from the mentor's knowledge, experience, and assistance. Profit and nonprofit organizations support these structured programs financially because they help employees develop personally and professionally as well as become more effective workers. This system is usually planned to last nine months, a year, or another specified period of time. This traditional system is described by the following characteristics:

- The mentor drives the relationship.
- Communication is primarily one way.
- The protégé benefits from the mentor's wisdom and experience.
- Other mentoring relationships and resources are often missed.
- The protégé may not get the full picture.
- Mentoring benefits may be limited.

In the diagram of closed-system mentoring, one can see the top-down relationship of the mentor and protégé, which once was called the "good old boys' network." Often, the CEOs or top executives in organizations are preparing the most promising employees to hold executive positions or even to replace themselves upon retirement. The one-way arrow from the mentor to the protégé denotes communication generally going one way. The circle encompassing the mentor and protégé is solid, blocking out other potential mentors and resources.

In most structured mentoring programs, an older, more experienced person will guide the development of a younger, less experienced individual. Such programs are highly applicable in planning formal mentoring programs in corporations, schools, youth organizations, government agencies, faith-based organizations, and other entities. Closed-system mentoring limits other resources, but examples of its success can be seen in accounts of informal mentoring from as far back as the sixth century BCE.

CLOSED

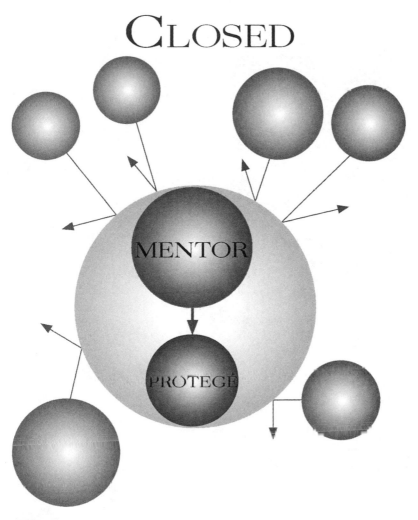

represents available mentoring resources

OPEN-SYSTEM MENTORING

Open-system mentoring can be incorporated into both formal and informal mentoring. For example, a protégé can be matched with a single mentor but be encouraged to "hunt and capture" as many mentors as needed to accomplish set goals. Individuals cultivate various mentoring relationships and numerous mentoring resources simultaneously and over time. In its finest form, the phenomenon of mentoring occurs naturally when protégés strive to fulfill their self-defined dreams. From a protégé's perspective, this enlarged idea of mentoring expands from accessing the wisdom of a single person to encompassing a variety of available assets. The open system can increase benefits for both parties and is described by the following characteristics:

- The protégé drives the mentoring relationship.
- The protégé is the leader of the mentoring environment.
- Mentoring relationships and resources are engaged simultaneously.
- Success is determined by the protégé's ability to seek, acquire, employ, and reengage valuable resources.

In the diagram of open-system mentoring, one can see how Richard's research changed the narrow definition of mentoring from top-down, mentor-driven mentoring to protégé-driven, multiple mentoring. The protégé is in the middle circle and singularly responsible for his or her success. The two-way arrows depict open communication among potential mentors and resources. The outer seven circles might represent an assigned mentor, such as a boss, supervisor, colleague, teacher, counselor, or even a "door opener," who made one significant phone call that changed everything. Notice that the encompassing circle is dotted, which can open to other galaxies of secondary resources, such as musicals, theater, music, works of art, and inspirational lives of family and historical figures, both living and dead.

Using his research project at Motorola to unearth this open version of mentoring, Richard made clear the specific, replicable characteristics of both systems: that was the essence of Richard's work in London. He took what he'd lived through and turned it into a scientific, evidence-based concept. He clarified his own thinking, made it accessible to others, and added to the body of empirical research on mentoring. He'd likely have used his own intuition in developing UIF, with or without this evidence, but his research could be a key factor in how UIF has grown, how readily its work has been adopted by others, and even whether it becomes as useful to humanity as Richard hoped.

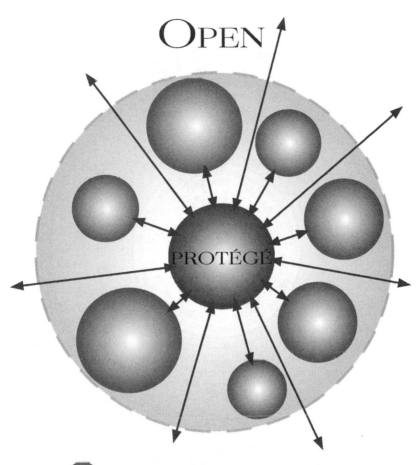

represents available mentoring resources

COLLABORATIVE-SYSTEM MENTORING

Collaborative-system mentoring incorporates many aspects of what Richard has called "natural" or "informal" mentoring. It's a group-oriented process where several individuals with the same goal, or complementary goals, act as if the others are mentoring resources. Leadership is shared and each participant shifts appropriately between the roles of mentor and mentee. The system can be highly effective, but it also can be problematic at times. Group dynamics can interfere with desired aims, and multiple resources might be difficult to manage. Collaborative-system mentoring can be described by the following characteristics:

- A group of individuals drives toward shared goals.
- Individuals act as each other's mentoring sources.
- Leadership is shared.
- Shared resources multiply among participants.
- Loss of one resource is less devastating on the whole.
- Group dynamics can interfere with the desired aims.
- Multiple resources can be difficult to manage.

In the diagram below, one can see the circles are different sizes representing the various strengths and skills of participants. There is no leader; each may act as a mentor or mentee at different times. Each arrow points both ways and crisscrosses to every participant, indicating that communication can flow like electrical currents with everyone participating in the discussion.

A good example of collaborative-system mentoring that John noticed occurred at the foundation. UIF's former chief operating officer was a student pilot who had not achieved his goal of becoming a licensed pilot. He began meeting with other student pilots. They combined their knowledge and resources and mentored each other to reach their common goal. Within two years, they had become certified pilots of small aircraft.

This system is highly applicable for entrepreneurs engaged in start-up ventures. It was especially true in 1989 when Richard started Integra LifeSciences with a handful of passionate people who reached their common goal of receiving FDA approval to market Integra™, the first commercially reproducible human skin.

COLLABORATIVE

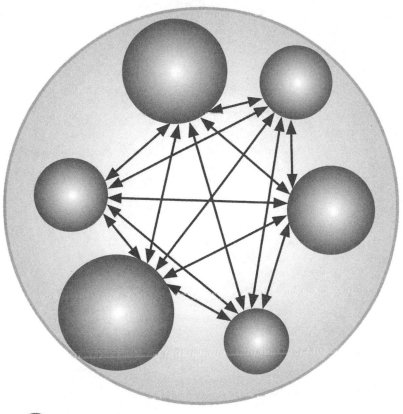

represents available mentoring resources

INSPIRATIONAL MENTORING RESOURCES

Richard Caruso believed that resources such as books, quotes, articles, poems, speeches, videos, music, dance, art, theater, and music can be significant mentors to young people and adults. Three examples of sayings, speeches, and poems that inspired Richard were printed in calligraphy, framed, and displayed in his office—*Attitude* by Charles Swindoll, *The Man in the Arena* by Theodore Roosevelt, and *If* by Rudyard Kipling.

ATTITUDE

By Dr. Charles Swindoll

The longer I live, the more I realize the impact of attitude on life. Attitude, to me, is more important than facts. It is more important than the past, than education, than money, than circumstances, than failures, than success, than what other people think, say or do. It is more important than appearance, giftedness, or skill. It will make or break a company . . . a church . . . a home. The remarkable thing is we have a choice every day regarding the attitude we will embrace for that day. We cannot change our past . . . we cannot change the fact that people will act in a certain way. We cannot change the inevitable. The only thing we can do is play on the one string we have, and that is our attitude. I am convinced that life is 10% what happens to me, and 90% how I react to it. And so it is with you . . . we are in charge of our Attitudes.

This passage, sometimes referred to as "The Man in the Arena," can be found on page seven of the thirty-five-page speech delivered by President Theodore Roosevelt at the Sorbonne in Paris, France, on April 23, 1910. It is the passage that made the speech famous.

THE MAN IN THE ARENA
By Theodore Roosevelt

It is not the critic who counts; not the man who points out how the strong man stumbles, or where the doer of deeds could have done them better. The credit belongs to the man who is actually in the arena, whose face is marred by dust and sweat and blood; who strives valiantly; who errs, who comes short again and again, because there is no effort without error and shortcoming; but who does actually strive to do the deeds; who knows great enthusiasms, the great devotions; who spends himself in a worthy cause; who at the best knows in the end the triumph of high achievement, and who at the worst, if he fails, at least fails while daring greatly, so that his place shall never be with those cold and timid souls who neither know victory nor defeat.

Rudyard Kipling wrote this poem in 1895 as if he were talking to his son. In one long sentence, he provided the young man a blueprint for living a stellar life.

If
By Rudyard Kipling

If you can keep your head when all about you
    Are losing theirs and blaming it on you;
If you can trust yourself when all men doubt you,
    But make allowance for their doubting too;
If you can wait and not be tired by waiting,
    Or being lied about, don't deal in lies,
Or being hated, don't give way to hating,
    And yet don't look too good, nor talk too wise;

If you can dream—and not make dreams your master;
    If you can think—and not make thoughts your aim;
If you can meet with triumph and disaster
    And treat those two impostors just the same;
If you can bear to hear the truth you've spoken
    Twisted by knaves to make a trap for fools,
Or watch the things you gave your life to broken,
    And stoop and build 'em up with worn-out tools;

If you can make one heap of all your winnings
    And risk it on one turn of pitch-and-toss,
And lose, and start again at your beginnings
    And never breathe a word about your loss;

If you can force your heart and nerve and sinew
  To serve your turn long after they are gone,
And so hold on when there is nothing in you
  Except the will which says to them: "Hold on";

If you can talk with crowds and keep your virtue,
  Or walk with kings—nor lose the common touch;
If neither foes nor loving friends can hurt you;
  If all men count with you, but none too much;
If you can fill the unforgiving minute
  With sixty seconds' worth of distance run—
Yours is the Earth and everything that's in it,
  And—which is more—you'll be a Man, my son!

THE FAILED EXPERIMENT

John Burke and Ioannis Yannas

When Richard Caruso finished his PhD in 1990 at the University of London, he became interested in finding a way to have humans regenerate their own organs and tissues. One day at UIF, Richard told John, "I'm no medical person, but I'm going to regenerate skin to save burn victims and regenerate other body parts."

John had told others that Richard was "cut from a different bolt of cloth," but this was crazy. John replied, "Rich, this is impossible," but he didn't know his partner was already on his way. The LFC board had canceled its unprofitable oil venture and medical start-up but had allowed Richard personally to buy the young medical company.

In reading various medical journals, Richard had learned that John F. Burke, MD of Harvard University, and Ioannis V. Yannas, PhD of Massachusetts Institute of Technology, were the inventors of a reproducible, synthetic human skin. He believed this improbable invention perfectly fit his sixth goal of the nine he had laid out: "Accomplish something that has never been done before." He traveled to Boston to see both of them.

Born in 1922 and a native of Chicago, John Burke was studying chemical engineering at the University of Illinois when World War II broke out, and he immediately volunteered for service.

When the war ended, he found his career goals had changed. He finished his undergraduate degree at the University of Illinois in 1947 and entered Harvard Medical School to earn his MD.

Early in his medical career, Burke made the treatment of badly burned patients his highest priority and the advancement of those treatments his personal quest. Ultimately, he became an eminent surgeon and chief of staff at the Shriners Burn Institute at Massachusetts General Hospital and especially had compassion for children who had been severely burned. Such was his dedication that during the catastrophic Northeastern United States blizzard of '78, Burke led a shovel brigade, clearing a path so that two badly burned boys could be brought in for treatment.

In 1969, having already made significant strides in burn treatment, he was still missing a piece of the puzzle. It occurred to him that he needed help—ironically, from a chemical engineer. He needed something to keep the bacteria out and keep the moisture in.

In his search, Burke brought his quest to a young assistant professor of polymer science and engineering at MIT. Ioannis V. Yannas, PhD, was recognized as one of the highest achievers in his field. He was born in Athens, Greece, in 1935. His father, Vassilios, co-owned a textile mill and a department store that sold woolen fabrics, while his mother worked at home and raised their three children.

In 1953, Yannas entered Harvard College, majoring in chemistry, and then earned an MS in chemical engineering at MIT in 1959. After working for a period in industrial research on polymers, Yannas earned his second master's degree and his PhD in physical chemistry at Princeton University in 1966.

When Burke shared a heartbreaking visit with Yannas to the pediatric burn ward at Shriners Burn Institute in Boston, it had a profound impact on Yannas. Over the next twelve years, they collaborated on the design of a flexible material that would protect the patient from infection and dehydration and not be rejected by the immune system. A range of synthetic and natural materials they tested on animals failed to speed up the healing process. When a final test with collagen polymers actually made healing slow down instead of speed up, the baffled scientists felt they had failed miserably. They began to think their quest to help burn victims was over. But they dug in to determine why.

What they discovered—a big surprise and hard to believe—was that while the healing was not accelerated as they had hoped, the test animals were not only growing the upper epidermis spontaneously but also growing the lower dermis, eventually leading to the development of a medical device: commercial name, Integra™.

As it turned out, Yannas's and Burke's skin did more than just block infection and retain moisture—it helped regenerate the dermal layer of skin without producing a scar. The trick was adding a synthetic layer of silicone on top of a layer of tissue-like scaffolding—a combination of molecular material from cow tendons and shark cartilage. The synthetic layer protects the skin from bacteria and infection and keeps the moisture in, while the collagen layer acts as a foundation on which new, healthy skin cells can grow. The breakthrough, as it happened, was the direct result of the failed experiment.

Burke and Yannas hesitated to publish their results, afraid no one would believe them. For years, they didn't understand the impact this discovery would have. They simply thought it was a new treatment for burn victims. Eventually, it became clear that they were regenerating a new organ (skin)—a groundbreaking model!

Finally, in 1981, they announced their success. Weaving together their collective expertise in engineered polymers and biology, they had created the first artificial skin. It was remarkable because it was well known that, once injured, the dermis never grows back by itself in adults; instead, the wounds fill with scar tissue.

Upon the announcement of this new product, Marion Laboratories in Kansas City bought the rights to the intellectual property from Harvard/MIT, with the approval of Dr. Burke and Dr. Yannas, to make the tissue-engineered skin. Marion Laboratories also agreed to conduct all the testing and conduct a clinical trial on the artificial skin. Before the synthetic skin could be used commercially, it had to be approved by the US Food and Drug Administration.

As this tedious process dragged on, Marion Labs became discouraged. During this time period, Marion was acquired by Merrell Dow Pharmaceuticals. The joint company became Marion Merrell Dow. The new owner arranged for Marion to continue several rounds of applying for FDA approval. After spending millions of dollars, Marion Merrell Dow felt the artificial skin was too new a technology for treatment of burn patients and that the FDA would never approve the skin. They decided to divest its subsidiary, Colla-Tec, which made the collagen for the artificial skin.

Having visited Dr. Burke and Dr. Yannas to learn how the artificial skin worked, Richard decided to take a calculated risk and try to buy the license. By then, it was back at Harvard/MIT, who told Richard they could not approve licensure of the artificial skin unless the inventors agreed. He went back to Burke and Yannas, who not only agreed to license their invention but also agreed to join Richard's team as consultants.

Richard then traveled to Marion Merrell Dow in Kansas City to buy the manufacturing equipment needed to make the artificial skin and buy Colla-Tec, which provided the critical collagen component of the product.

Testing the UIF model of collaborative-system mentoring, Richard assembled a formidable team: Frederick Cahn, a PhD from MIT who was already working with Richard to create another medical start-up; Judi O'Grady, a high-level regulatory affairs employee at Colla-Tec, subsidiary of Marion Merrell Dow, with experience and expertise with FDA; and even the inventors, John Burke and Ioannis Yannas. Having no medical background, Richard had assembled mentoring partners who collectively were experts in every aspect of his goal.

Seven years after Richard started his company, Integra Life-Sciences, and had spent millions of his own money, the FDA finally approved Integra Artificial Skin in 1996! The Burke-Yannas synthetic skin then reached the commercial market and has been a lifesaver for thousands of patients throughout the world—not just those fighting extensive burns, but also those needing reconstruction and those with chronic wound diseases.

Dr. John F. Burke, professor of surgery emeritus, who in 1969 began a long research partnership with a young MIT professor of mechanical and biological engineering that led to the development of the first commercially reproducible, synthetic human skin, died In November 2011 at the age of eighty-nine.

Dr. Ioannis V. Yannas, who partnered with Dr. Burke to invent the artificial skin, Integra™, currently holds a joint appointment in the mechanical engineering department and the biological engineering department at MIT. He teaches classes in biomaterials-tissue Interactions, cell-matrix mechanics, and design of medical devices and implants.

John Burke and Ioannis Yannas have been honored with numerous awards, and both were inducted into the 2015 National Inventors Hall of Fame, joining the five hundred renowned Hall-of-Fame inventors, such as the Wright Brothers and Steve Jobs.

Richard E. Caruso, PhD, founder of UIF in 1986 and Integra LifeSciences in 1989, has received multiple awards and was named the 2006 Ernst & Young Greater Philadelphia Entrepreneur of the Year and the 2006 Entrepreneur of the Year for the United States of America.

John C. Crosby, EdD
November 2018

A LIST OF RECOMMENDED BOOKS

SCHOLARLY BOOKS ON MENTORING
Theory, Research, Principles, and Practice

Blanchard, Ken, and Claire Diaz-Ortiz. *One Minute Manager: How to Find and Work with a Mentor—and Why You'll Benefit from Being One.* New York: William Morrow, 2017.

Carreau, Debby. *The Mentoring Myth: How to Take Control of Your Own Success.* New York: Routledge, 2016.

Caruso, Richard E. *Mentoring and the Business Environment: Asset or Liability?* London: Dartmouth, 1992.

Clutterbuck, David. *Everyone Needs a Mentor.* 4th ed. London: Institute of Personnel and Development, 2008.

Collins, James. *Mentors: Noted Dartmouth Alumni Reflect on the Teachers Who Changed Their Lives.* Hanover, NH: Dartmouth College Press, 1991.

Cottrell, David. *Monday Morning Mentoring: Ten Lessons to Guide You up the Ladder.* New York: HarperCollins, 2008.

Damon, William. *The Path to Purpose: How Young People Find Their Calling in Life.* New York: Free Press, 2009.

Emelo, Randy. *Modern Mentoring.* Alexandria, VA: ATD Press. 2015.

Engstrom, Ted W. *The Fine Art of Mentoring: Passing on to Others What God Has Given to You.* With Norman B. Rohrer. Brentwood, TN: Wolgemuth & Hyatt, 1989.

Freedman, Marc. *The Kindness of Strangers: Adult Mentors, Urban Youth, and the New Voluntarism.* Paperback ed. Cambridge, UK: University of Cambridge Press, 1999.

Greenewalt, Crawford H. *The Uncommon Man: The Individual in the Organization*. New York: McGraw Hill, 1959.

Hendricks, Howard G., and William D. Hendricks. *As Iron Sharpens Iron: Building Character in a Mentoring Relationship*. 2nd ed. Chicago: Moody, 1999.

Homer. *The Odyssey*. Translated by Emily Wilson. New York: W. W. Norton, 2018.

Huang, Chungliang Al, and Jerry Lynch. *Tao Mentoring: Cultivate Collaborative Relationships in All Areas of Your Life*. New York: HarperCollins, 1999.

Johnson, W. Brad, and Charles R. Ridley. *The Elements of Mentoring: 75 Practices of Master Mentors*. Rev. ed. New York: St. Martin's Press, 2008.

Johnson, W. Brad, and David Smith. *Athena Rising: How and Why Men Should Mentor Women*. New York: Routledge, 2018.

Kreider, Larry. *Authentic Spiritual Mentoring*. Ventura, CA: Regal, 2008.

Labin, Jenn. *Mentoring Programs That Work*. Rochester, NY: Association for Talent Development, 2017.

Levinson, Daniel J. *The Seasons of a Man's Life*. With Charlotte N. Darrow, Edward B. Klein, Maria H. Levinson, and Braxton McKee. New York: Ballantine Books, 1978.

Levinson, Daniel J., in collaboration with Judy D. Levinson. *The Seasons of a Woman's Life*. New York: Ballantine Books, 1996.

Maxwell, John C., *Mentoring 101: What Every Leader Needs to Know*. New York: HarperCollins Leadership, 2008.

Phillips-Jones, Linda. *Mentors & Protégés: How to Establish, Strengthen and Get the Most from a Mentoring/Protégé Relationship*. 2nd ed. Grass Valley, CA: Coalition of Counseling Centers / The Mentoring Group, 2001.

Ragins, Bell Rose, and Kathy E. Kram, eds. *The Handbook of Mentoring at Work: Theory, Research and Practice*. Thousand Oaks, CA: Sage, 2007.

Rath, Tom. *StrengthsFinders 2.0*. New York: Gallup Press, 2007.

Rhodes, Jean E. *Stand by Me: The Risks and Rewards of Mentoring Today's Youth*. Cambridge, MA: Harvard University Press, 2002.

Sheehy, Gail. *New Passages*. New York: Ballantine Books, 1996.

Wellington, Sheila. *Be Your Own Mentor: Strategies from Top Women on the Secrets of Success*. With Betty Spence. New York: Random House, 2001.

BOOKS WITH EXAMPLES OF NATURAL MENTORING
Autobiography, Biography, Memoir, and Nonfiction

Agassi, Andre. *Open: An Autobiography*. New York: Vintage Books, 2010.

Albom, Mitch. *Tuesdays with Morrie: An Old Man, a Young Man, and Life's Greatest Lesson*. New York: Doubleday, 1997.

Ashe, Arthur, and Arnold Rampersad. *Days of Grace: A Memoir*. New York: Alfred A. Knopf, 1993.

Blauner, Andres, ed. *Coach: 25 Writers Reflect on People Who Made a Difference*. New York: Time Warner Book Group, 2005.

Brooks, David. *The Road to Character*. New York: Random House, 2015.

Brooks, David. *The Second Mountain*. New York: Random House, 2019.

Brown, Brené. *Daring Greatly: How the Courage to Be Vulnerable Transforms the Way We Live, Love, Parent, and Lead*. New York: Gotham Books, 2012.

Clifton, Donald O., and Paula Nelson. *Soar with Your Strengths*. New York: Dell, 1992.

Couric, Katie. *The Best Advice I Ever Got: Lessons from Extraordinary Lives*. New York: Random House, 2011.

Cuomo, Matilda Raffa, ed. *The Person Who Changed My Life: Prominent People Recall Their Mentors*. 2nd ed. New York: Barnes & Noble Books, 2002.

Duckworth, Angela. *Grit: The Power of Passion and Perseverance*. New York: Scribner, 2018.

Duhigg, Charles. *The Power of Habit: Why We Do What We Do in Life and Business*. New York: Random House, 2012.

Dungy, Tony. *The Mentor Leader: Secrets to Building People and Teams That Win Consistently*. With Nathan Whitaker. Carol Stream, IL: Tyndale House, 2010.

Edelman, Marian Wright. *The Measure of Our Success: A Letter to My Children and Yours*. Boston: Beacon Press, 1992.

Edelman, Marian Wright. *Lanterns: A Memoir of Mentors*. Boston: Beacon Press, 1999.

King, Maxwell. *The Good Neighbor: The Life and Work of Fred Rogers*. New York: Harry N. Abrams, 2018.

Lewis, Michael. *The Blind Side*. New York: W. W. Norton, 2007.

Lopez, Steve. *The Soloist: A Lost Dream, an Unlikely Friendship, and the Redemptive Power of Music*. New York: Berkley, 2008.

McCullough, David. *John Adams*. New York: Simon & Schuster, 2001.

Moore, Wes. *The Other Wes Moore: One Name, Two Fates*. New York: Spiegel & Grau, 2011.

Orfalea, Paul, and Ann Marsh. *Copy This! Lessons from a Hyperactive Dyslexic Who Turned a Bright Idea into One of America's Best Companies*. New York: Workman, 2005.

Pausch, Randy. *The Last Lecture*. With Jeffrey Zaslow. New York: Hyperion, 2008.

Rogers, Fred. *The World According to Mister Rogers: Important Things to Remember*. New York: Hyperion, 2003.

Sandberg, Sheryl. *Lean In: Women, Work, and the Will to Lead*. New York: Alfred A. Knopf, 2013.

Sotomayor, Sonia. *My Beloved World*. New York: Vintage Books, 2013.

Suskind, Ron. *A Hope of the Unseen: An American Odyssey from the Inner City to the Ivy League*. New York: Broadway Books, 1998.

Thomas, Marlo, ed. *The Right Words at the Right Time*. New York: Atria Books, 2002.

Thomas, Marlo, Bruce Kluger, Carl Robbins, and David Tabatsky. *The Right Words at the Right Time*. Vol. 2, *Your Turn!* New York: Atria Books, 2006.

Westover, Tara. *Educated: A Memoir*. New York: Random House, 2018.

Wiltshire, Susan Ford. *Athena's Disguises: Mentors in Everyday Life*. Louisville, KY: Westminster John Knox, 1998.

Wooden, John, and Jack Tobin. *They Call Me Coach*. New York: Contemporary Books, 1988.

Wooden, John, and Don Yaeger. *A Game Plan of Life: The Power of Mentoring*. New York: Bloomsbury USA, 2009.

INDEX

Page numbers in italics refer to figures.

Abilene Christian University, 74–75, *124*
accolades, 129
accomplishments. *See* success
accounting, 24–29, 59, 105–14
achieving goals, 77, *79*
Ackerman, Rudy S., 21, 50
acquisition of products, 112, 119
actions, changes in, 94–95
addiction, 32–33
admiration, mutual, 76–77
advice, 77–78
affirmation, verbal, 123
aging population, 93
Aiken, David, 10, 22, 136
Akamu, Nina, 50
Allentown Art Museum, 21, 50
altar boy, 5
alternative energy, 93
American Capital Mutual Funds, 120
American College, 68
American Dream, 161
Amtrak, 37
analyzing businesses, 105–6
anger, at injustice, 91
Anido, Bonnie Caruso, x, 57–58, 59, 108, 134
animals, mentoring behaviors of, 73
anxiety, 77
apartments, off-campus, 22–23, 129
appreciation, importance of, 106
apps, creation of, 151

Architectural Digest, 117–18
Arduini, Peter, 125
Army Reserve, 27, 31–34, 85
art, importance of, x, 21, 49, 175–76, 183
artificial skin, 97–112, 189–92
Ash Wednesday Storm, 17
assigned mentors, 89
Athens, Greece, 190
Atlantic City, New Jersey, xi, 3, 41
Atlantic City Convention Center, 7
Atlantic City High School, 10, 11, 15
at-risk students, 67
Attitude (Swindoll), 183–84
attitudes, changes in, 94–95
auditing, 29, 111
authoritarianism, 9
awards, 111, 121, 93, 127, 193

baby boomers, aging, 93
balanced partnerships, 24
bankruptcy, 139
baseball, 51–52, 58–59, 101
Baskerville, Meghan, 160
Basvapatri, Sravya, 152
Baum, Russell, 20–26, 49–50, 65–70, 75–77, 131
Baum, Walter Emerson, 21, 50, 57
Baumfolder Corporation, 21
Baum School of Art, 21, 50
beach houses, 53
beauty, importance of, 22

Bellino, Joe, 20

Bellmawr, New Jersey, 32

benefits to humanity, 61, 85, 93, 115, 125, 167

betting, on horse races, 84–85

Biemic Society, 31

biomimicry, 94

blame, 186

Blessed Sacrament School, 9

blessings, 75

boardwalks, repair of, 19

Bongard, Jennifer. *See* Caruso, Jennifer Bongard

Boston, Massachusetts, 37

Boston Scientific, 108

Boyd, John, 14, 65–68, 131

Bradley, Keith, xi, 107

brain, elasticity of, 95

breaking away, 77–78, *79*

Brown, Barbara, 47

Brown, Cassidy, 151

Brown, Herb, x, 3, 47, 121

Bryn Mawr, Pennsylvania, 68

Bucknell University, 26, 75, 123, 151

Buddhism, 72

bullying, 10–11, 49

Burdo, Joe, 163

Burke, John F., 97–109, 189–94

burn patients, 98–99, 189–91

business development, 148–49

business management, 152

Business Performance Group, 107, 120

bus stops. *See* school bus stops

Cable News Network (CNN), 35

Cahn, Frederick, 100, 192–93

calcium supplements, 101

calculated risks. *See* risk management

calculating numbers, 47–48

Camel City Solar, 121

cameras, purchase of, 9

Camp Sunshine, 12

Capo d'Orlando, Sicily, 3

caregivers, xi, 136

Carnahan, Joanna, ix–x

carpentry, 73

Caruso, Bonnie. *See* Anido, Bonnie Caruso

Caruso, Carmen, x, 4, 11, 22, 33–34, 47, 132–34

Caruso, Charles, 26

Caruso, Christopher, 22

Caruso, Cono Sarafino, v, 3–4, 9, 18–19, 33–34, 40–44, 60–63, 127, 132, 139

Caruso, Frances. *See* Holtz, Frances Caruso

Caruso, Jennifer Bongard, 117

Caruso, John, 34

Caruso, Jonathan, x–xi, 39, 44–47, 53–59, 83–87, 105–7, 117, 126, 133

Caruso, Joseph, x, 4, 9, 20, 44, 51, 59, 132–34

Caruso, Kaitlyn, 117, 126

Caruso, Kristin. *See* Clark, Kristin Caruso

Caruso, Louise (Louisa) Pirolli, v, 3–5, 18–19, 33–34, 40, 132

Caruso, Peter, x–xi, 39–40, 43–44, 53–58, 87, 107, 133

Caruso, Richard Ernest Joseph: auditing job, 29; awards received by, 121–23, 127–29; birth of, 4; comfortable life earned by, 132; contradictory traits, 137; determination, 102; donations made by, 134; football played by, 10, 17, 23–26; on happiness, 29; helping others, 131; marriage, 38–39; nine goals, 167; parenting, 39–42; summer jobs, 12; suspension from school, 17–18; Uncommon Individual Foundation started by, ix; understanding of mentoring, 71; vision, 102; work experience, 30

Caruso, Sally Feitig, v, x, 24, 38–39, 43–47, 53–58, 84–87, 95–96, 107, 118–27, 134

Catholicism, 39

Cawsl Corporation, 45

CeeLite Technologies, LLC, 121

celebrations, 109

Census Bureau, US, 75

Center for Economics, Business, and Entrepreneurship Education, Susquehanna University, 162

Certified Public Accountants (CPA), 30, 34

Charles, Prince, 53–54
Charles A. Melton Center, 157
chemical engineering, 190
ChemoCozy, 149–50
Chester Springs, Pennsylvania, 54, 91
children: supporting, 42; taking to work, 54
China, 88
choices: attitude as, 183–84; importance of, 5–6
Cirque du Soleil, 122
citizenship, 101
Claiborne Farm, 91
Clark, Kristin Caruso, x, 134
Clark, Monica, 152
class size, 56, 73
closed-system mentoring, x, 90, 171–73, *173*
clothing, modest, 15
CNN. *See* Cable News Network (CNN)
coaching, 15–16, 58–59, 145
coal fired plants, 48–49
Cohen, Alan (Pencil), 10–11
coin-flipping game, 29
collaboration, 26, 35, 73, 97–98, 133, 162
collaborative-system mentoring, 179–81, *181*
collagen, 98–100, 108, 118, 191–92
Colla-Tec, 100–108, 192–93
college: money for, 11, 14, 41, 154; researching, 154
Collins Foods, 59
Colmey, James, 75
commitment to good, 102
communication: multidirectional, 179; one-way, 171; open, 175; skills, 77
communities: farming, 73; mentor-rich, 136–37; support for, 101
compassion, 139
competition, 81–82
computer-equipment companies, 36–37
computers, 47–48, 121
confidence, 59, 96, 106, 144
confidences, sharing of, 77
conflicts, handling, 64
Confucianism, 72
connections, personal, 9, 115
Conner, Chris, 111

Conner, Dana Holtz, 33, 39, 53, 57–58, 92, 96, 107, 111
construction jobs, 19–21
Consumer Reports, 64
contractors, building, 115
contradictions, personal, 137
contribution, human need for, 69
Cooley, Michael, 131
cooperation, 70, 81–82
coordinators, 169
core training workshops, 170
core values, 88
Cornell University, 51–52
Cornerstone Christian Academy, 159
corporate mentoring, 142–47, 169–70
courage, 105
coursework requirements, 85
CPA. *See* Certified Public Accountants (CPA)
craniosacral therapy, 126
creativity, 7–8, 35, 144
Crenny, Kathleen, xi, 126
criticism: avoidance of, 74; constructive, 150
Crosby, John C., 17, 54, 64–65, 71, 85–86, 119–27, 133–47, 189
Crosby, Marlene, xii
cruise ships, 47
culture: institutional, 69; of mentoring, 120
curiosity, 10, 31
cystic fibrosis, 91

Dale, Rachel, 54–55
Dallas Cowboys, 14
D'Amato, Paul (Skinny), 10–11
da Vinci, Leonardo, 50
Davis, Sammy, 11
dehydration, 98, 191
DeJesus, James, 115
Delaware, State of, 143
delivery trucks, 24
dementia, 126, 136
Denver Seminary, 147
dermis, 191–92
determination, 5, 81, 105–6. *See also* perseverance

developing relationships, 77, *79*

development: business, 148–49; personal, 6; professional, 70, 171

developmental stages, 78

Devon, Pennsylvania, 142, 151

DiAntonio, Chris, xii, 150, 158

Diasome Pharmaceuticals, 120

Di-Francesco, Ben, 25

dignity of work, 19

DiLella, Gary, xi, 44–45, 132–33

disagreements, working through, 77

Distinguished Alumni Citation, Abilene Christian University, 124

diverse workforce, 69

divorce, 33

documentaries, 162

dog, purchase of, 8–9

donations, 134

doubt, 186

Dow Chemical, 67, 99, 143

dreams: helping others realize, 164–65; importance of, 186; personal, 7–8; of protégés, 76, 77, 89; pursuit of, 66; self-defined, 175

Drexel University, 123

drinking alcohol, 129

DuPont, 29–30, 66, 143

DuraGen, 118–19

dura mater, 118–19

Dwyer, Betsy, xii, 156

Eastern Interconnection grid, 36

education: importance of, 64–65, 88, 105–6, 152–57; mentoring, 152–57; public, 54–57; science education, 67

effort, importance of, 185

Egg Harbor, New Jersey, 134

elasticity, of brain, 95

e-learning, 152–57

Electronic Data Systems, 138

Eli Lilly, 143

Elisio, Christina, 159

eMarketer, 160

emotional intelligence, 77, 123

EMP. *See* Entrepreneur Mentoring Program (EMP)

empathy, 5, 8, 40–42, 114–15, 139

employees, attracting, 69

empowerment, 8

E. M. Stanton School, 156–57

encouragement, 149–50

energy, alternative, 83

engineering, mentoring in, 158–60

enrichment, personal, 35

enthusiasm, 12

entrepreneurial philanthropy, 149

Entrepreneurial Summit, Bucknell, 123

Entrepreneur Mentoring Program (EMP), 147–52

Entrepreneur of the Year for the United States of America, 122, 194

entrepreneurship, 30, 45, 120, 123–24, 152

epidermis, 191

epigenetics, 94

ePlanet Ventures III, 120

equal relationships, 78

equipment leasing, 30, 36–37, 83, 121

Ernst & Young Greater Philadelphia Entrepreneur of the Year, 121, 147, 194

Ernst & Young National Award in Health Sciences, 122

error, effort and, 185

essence, personal, 130

Essig, Stuart, xi, 112–14, 119, 125, 133

evaluation, of mentoring programs, 170

Evins, Joe L., 75

Ewing Marion Kauffman Foundation, 101

"Examination of Organizational Mentoring, An" (Caruso), 89

excellence, pride in, 117

Exelon Corporation, 36

failure, 8, 138

faith, 105

family: vacations, 57–58, 87–88; value of, 42, 134, 135

farming communities, 73

father figures, 39–40

favoritism, 135

FDA. *See* Food and Drug Administration, US (FDA)

FedEx, 35

Feitig, Sally. *See* Caruso, Sally Feitig

financial literacy, 88
financial success, 61, 167
firing employees, 137
First Sterling Bank, 120
500 Club, 10–11
Fleur de Lis racing stable, 84
flexibility: in education, 20; importance of, 25; in mentoring, 70
focus group sessions, 170
food, organic and local, 91
Food and Drug Administration, US (FDA), 99–113, 192–93
football, 10, 17, 23–26, 131, 136
Forgerson, Roger, 22–23
formal mentoring, 171–73, *173*, 175
freedom, personal, 6–8, 16–18, 22–25, 77–78, 130–31
freight trains, 37
Freschi, Nic, 150–51
Fretz, Mark, xii
friendships, 13, 24, 78, 90, 118, 135, 145–46
frugality, 3, 8–9, 58, 74, 92, 96, 116
Fry, Douglas, 74–75

gambling, 11, 32–33
Garrett, James W., 14, 17–19, 23–26, 65, 74–75, 125, 131, 163
Garrett, Jason, 14
gas stations, 24
General Motors, 138
generosity, 32–33, 92
George Mason University, 111
Germany, 88
Gino's restaurants, 46
goals: achieving, 77; articulation of, 90; career, 60, clarifying, 170; focus on, 52; lofty, 95; long-term, 22; nine goals, 61, 64, 81, 167; of organizations, 70; passion in pursuit of, 90; personal, 61, 70; self-determination of, 29, 80; shared, 25, 170, 179; of Uncommon Individual Foundation, 81
Goldman Sachs, 113
good old boys' network, 172
graduate school, 26
graduation, high school, 14, 153
grafts, skin, 98

Granville Avenue School, 9
gratitude, 68–69, 151
Green, Helen, ix
Greenewalt, Crawford H., 63, 66
group dynamics, 25, 76, 179
growth, professional and personal, 90
guidance, 77
Gunkel, Naomi, xii

Hackman, Michael, xii, 133, 150–54
Haines, Henry, x, 31, 38–39, 69, 75
Hames, Charles, xii
Hamilton, Ellen, 149–50
Hamilton College, 151
happiness, mentoring and, 81
hard work, 72–73, 130
Harvard University, 97–100, 190–92
Hayes, Sarae Black, 146
Hayes-Arrington, Deloris, 145
Heard, Christine, xii, 145
heart transplants, 94
helping: accepting help, 137; financially struggling people, 30; human need for, 69, 82; importance of, 131; one-way help, 72; value of, 16, 61; vision of, 70
hierarchy, organizational, 97, 122
high-functioning relationships, 135
high-speed trains, 37
Hirsch, Dick, 22–23
Holtz, Dana. *See* Conner, Dana Holtz
Holtz, David, 27, 39–41, 53, 85, 113–14, 133
Holtz, Frances Caruso, v, x, 4, 14–15, 22–27, 32–33, 40–42, 69, 132
Holtz, Jerry, xi, 24, 39–41, 51–52, 78, 92, 108, 126, 132–36
Holtz, Nicholas, 52
home improvements, 54
Homer, 72
homework support, 156
honesty, 48, 72–73
horse business, x, 53–54, 84, 91, 135
hospitalization, 112
hubcaps, stealing, 11
humanity, benefits to, 61, 85, 93, 107–8, 115, 125, 167
humor, 85

iBalans, 150

IBM. *See* International Business Machines (IBM)

ice cream, 7–8, 42

If (Kipling), 186–87

"I Have a Dream" (King), 66

I Have a Dream Foundation, 67

imagination, 7–8

incubator programs, 149

independence. *See* freedom, personal

individual needs, 25

Infante, Charles, 67

infections, 98, 191

informal mentoring, 172–79

initiative, 5, 90, 130

injustice, anger at, 91

innovation, 164

Innovation Competition, Susquehanna University, 163

institutional knowledge, 69

instructions, standardized, 102

insurance industry, 112

Integra LifeSciences, xi–xii, 100–25, 133–35, 180, 191–93

intellectual challenges, 61, 93, 167

Interactive Investor International, 120

International Business Machines (IBM), 36–37, 143

interns, 151–52

intuition, 130

investment: creating pathways to, 148; funding, 107

iReady computer-based education modules, 156–57

Islam, 72

Italy, 3, 57–58, 88

Ithan Elementary School, 56

JJ's Joy, 84

Johnson and Johnson, 108

Jones, Mary Catherine, 151

Kansas City, xii, 100–103

Kansas City Royals, 101

Kauffman, Ewing Marion, 93, 100–103, 116, 122

Kenny, Marty, 163–64

Kickstarter campaigns, 163

kindness, 114–15

King, Martin Luther, 66

King of Prussia, Pennsylvania, 39, 46–49

Kipling, Rudyard, 186–87

Kirksey, Shakia, xii, 154

knowledge: combination of, 179–80; institutional, 69

Kirtan Kriya, 126

Lafrentz & Co., 26

Land, Thomas P., 68, 87–89

landscaping, 13

layers of meaning, 71

leadership, shared, 179

leading-edge technology, 61, 93, 167

learning: continuous, 29; lifelong, 88

Lease Financing Corporation (LFC), x, 30–37, 44–48, 60, 83–85, 96, 103, 138–39

leasing: computers, 36–37; equipment, 30, 83, 121; paintings, 50; real estate, 44; ships, 47

Leno, Jay, 122

Leonardo's Horse, 50

LFC. *See* Lease Financing Corporation (LFC)

LFC Lifesciences, 85

Liberty Folding Company, 20–21

Liguori Academy, 159

limited partnerships, 44

linoleum, replacement of, 33–34

literacy, 73, 152–57

Little League, 58–59

local food, 91

London School of Economics, x, xi, 86, 92, 107, 120, 189

long-distance telephone calls, 35–36

Lopez, Joseph, xii, 133, 148–50

Lopez, Lucy, xii, 150, 161

Lord, Jack, 55

loss, recovery from, 187

loyalty, 144

luck, 75

luncheon celebrations, 71

luxury, 58

MacLean, Robbie, 126
Main Line, 21
Malcolm X. *See* X, Malcolm
management, business, 152
"Man in the Arena, The" (Roosevelt), 185
Manzi, Italo, x, 108, 115–18, 133–35
Manzi, Phyllis, 117
March on Washington (1963), 66
Margate, New Jersey, 8 10, 22–24, 32–33, 39–43
Marion Laboratories, xii, 97–104, 192
marketing, defining messages, 161
market research, 151
marriage, life lessons of, 42
Marriott, Bill, 59–60
Marriott, Richard, 46
Marriott Corporation, 46–47, 59–60
Marrone, Michael, 160
Massachusetts General Hospital, 98, 190
Massachusetts Institute of Technology (MIT), 97–100, 190–93
master of science in business administration (MSBA), 26
matching mentors to mentees, 71
mathematics, mentoring in, 158–60
McCaffery, Barbara, 143–44
McCarthy, Jake, 55
McCormick, Felix, 75
McCoy, Jill, 146
MCI. *See* Microwave Communications Incorporated (MCI)
Media Mentoring Program (MMP), 160–64
medical devices, 31, 85
medical protocols, 102
medical research, 93
Medici Archive Project, 120
medicine, regenerative, 119
meditation, 126
memories, writing down, 125–26
Men's Judiciary Board, Susquehanna University, 17
Mentor, 72, 80
mentoring: advantages of, 107–8; advice and, 77; alternative sources of, 89; animal behavior and, 73; assigned mentors, 89; benefits of, 76; for biotech

hires, 125; closed-system mentoring, x, 90, 96, 171–73, *173*; collaborative-system mentoring, 96–98, 179–81, *181*, 192–93; community, 136–37, 149; corporate, 142–47, 169–70; culture of, 107–8, 120; definition of, 68–69, 132; development of mentors, 164–65; education, 152–57; of entrepreneurs, 147–52; evaluation of programs, 170; family and, *135*; focus of, 16; formal, 171–73, *173*, 175; groups benefitting from, 76; guidance, 77; happiness and, 81; informal, 172–75, 179; innovation in, 164; literacy program, 156–57; matching mentors to mentees, 71; media mentoring, 160–64; multiple mentors, x, 72, 76, 170, 175; natural, 14–16, 21, 24–26, 88–90, 179; one-on-one mentoring, x, 69, 87, 170; open-system mentoring, x, 90, 96; organizational, 89; outreach programs in, 133; programs designed for, 67, 169–70; protégé-driven, 87, 145, 175; qualifications for, 90; redefinition of, 124; relationships, 76, *79*; in religious texts, 72; research, 176; reverse, 104; in science, technology, engineering, and mathematics, 158–60; strength through, 153; structured, 87–90, 141–47, 169–73, *173*; study of, 85–86; success and, 81; symposium on, 67–69, 87; teaching of, 132; three systems of, 171–81; use of word, 67; videos about, 161
"Mentoring: How Are You Doing?" (UIF), 170
Mentoring and the Business Environment (Caruso), 107
Mentors-in-Residence (MIR), 164
mentorsphere, 80
Merion Station, Pennsylvania, 21, 24
Merrell Dow Pharmaceuticals, 99, 192
Metroliner trains, 37
Microwave Communications Incorporated (MCI), 35–36
Mid-Atlantic Capital Alliance Award, 123
Midland, Michigan, 67
MIR. *See* Mentors-in-Residence (MIR)
mission, of Uncommon Individual Foundation, 66, 141

mistakes, fixing, 116
MIT. *See* Massachusetts Institute of Technology (MIT)
MMP. *See* Media Mentoring Program (MMP)
mobile devices, time spent on, 160
modest clothing, 15
money, saving. *See* frugality
Monte Carlo, 122
Motorola, 68, 87–89, 122, 143, 176
Mount Carmel, New Jersey, 124
movie theaters, 13
MSBA. *See* master of science in business administration (MSBA)
Muir, Bill, x, 23–25, 85–86, 124
multimedia studios, 161
multiple mentors, x, 72, 175, 179
Muolo, Mary, x
Museum of the American Revolution, 120
mutual admiration, 76–77, 79
mutual benefits, 68
mutual goals. *See* goals: shared
mutual relationships, 77

NASDAQ, 110
National Football League (NFL), 23
National Inventors Hall of Fame, 193
National Italian American Foundation (NIAF), 126
natural mentoring, 14–16, 21–26, 88–90, 179
Naval Academy, US, 20
Nehru, Jawaharlal, 129
nerves, regeneration of, 118–19
networking, 68
NeuroGen, 118–19
NeuroTinker, 163
New Jersey Entrepreneurial Leadership Award in Biomaterial Science, 121
New Jersey Science Teachers Association, 12
newspapers, selling, 7–8, 24
NewSpring Capital, 120
Newsweek, 67
New Testament, 72
New York Central Railroad, 37

New York City, 37
New York Giants, 14
NFL. *See* National Football League (NFL)
NIAF. *See* National Italian American Foundation (NIAF)
Nichols, Joe, 108, 112, 115, 133
nine goals, 61, 64, 81, 167
nonprofit foundations, 65
Notable Breakthrough Device award, 111
nudist colonies, 12
nursing homes, 50

Oak Ridge School District, 147
Ocean City, New Jersey, 53
Odysseus, 72
Odyssey, The, 72
O'Grady, Judi, xii, 103–12, 125, 133, 193
Old Testament, 72
Ollinger, Richard, 159
one-on-one mentoring, x, 69, 87, 170
one-way relationships, 76–78
online learning, 152–57
OnTrack to Post-Secondary Education, 152–55
ON/UP Philadelphia, 162
open-system mentoring, x, 90, 175–77, 177
opportunities, creation of, 19, 44, 61, 115, 167
organic food, 91
organizational hierarchy, 122
organizations, 63–64
organ transplants, 94
orientation meetings, 169
outreach programs, 133
overnight delivery services, 34–35

paintings, leasing of, 50
Palm Springs, California, 122
parenting, 39, 106
Paris, France, 185
partnership-centric programs, 156
passion, importance of, 81, 90, 123
Peabody College of Vanderbilt University, 75

PECO. *See* Philadelphia Electric Company (PECO)

Penn Central Transportation Company, 37

Pennsylvania-New Jersey-Maryland Interconnection (PJM), 36

Pennsylvania Railroad, 37

performance, assessment of, 70

perseverance, 72–73, 76, 103–5, 131. *See also* determination

personal growth, 70, 90

personal help, 115

petitions, 18–19

Phail, Evan, xii

Philadelphia, Pennsylvania, 21, 161–62

Philadelphia Electric Company (PECO), 36

Philadelphia Elementary Principal Intern Program, 146–47

Philadelphia Inquirer, 69

Philadelphia Park racetrack, 84

Philadelphia Phillies, 51

philanthropy, entrepreneurial, 149

Phoenix Steel, 138–39

physical labor, 14, 40

Pietrzyk, Ben, xii, 144, 150

Pignatore, John, x, 22–23, 129

pilot certification, 179–80

pinball, 6

Pirolli, Louise. *See* Caruso, Louise Pirolli

Pittello, Robert, 15–17, 25–26, 59, 65, 124–25, 131, 163

PJM. *See* Pennsylvania-New Jersey-Maryland Interconnection (PJM)

planning sessions, 144, 169

PNC. *See* Provident National Corporation (PNC)

Poconos, 38

policy, public, 112

polymers, 98, 190

pooling costs, 36

popularity, 69

posttraumatic stress disorder, 163–64

potential, assessment of, 70

potential, personal, 130

Potter, Michelle, 144

power, sharing, 97

power-over strategies, 97, 118

power-with idea, 49

pranks, 18–19

Price Waterhouse, 29–34, 113

pride, 117

Princeton University, 95, 190

private funding, 107

problem solving, 74, 95–96, 102, 116

professional growth, 70, 90

program heads, 71

Project Choice, 101

promotion of employees, 70

protégé-driven mentoring, 76–81, 87–90, 175

Protestantism, 39

protocols, medical, 102

Provco Group Ltd., xi, 44–45, 60, 78, 108, 117–20, 126, 132–36

Provident National Corporation (PNC), 45

P.S. 121, East Harlem, 66

public companies, 113–14

public education, 54–57

public speaking, 146

Quaker BioVentures, 120

qualifications, for mentoring, 90

questionnaires, 170

rabbi, meaning of word, 72

race horses, 84–85

Radius Book Group, xii

Radnor, Pennsylvania, 87, 93, 142

Radnor Corporate Center, 142

Radnor School District, 54, 64

rags-to-riches stereotype, 132

railroad companies, 37

reading people, 130

Reagan, Ronald, 64

real estate leasing, 44

rebellion, 106

reciprocity, culture of, 70

reconstructing corporations, 37

REC Studio, 161–62

regeneration of body parts, 95, 102, 109, 118, 189–91

regenerative medicine, 109, 119
Regulatory Affairs, 104
Reinhart Food Service, 124
relationships: developing, 77; equal, 78;
    high-functioning, 135; mutual, 77;
    one-way, 76–78; patterns in, 76
religious texts, mentoring in, 72
repair: of buildings, 19; of cars, 11, 13; of
    medical devices, 31, 85
research: of colleges, 154; medical, 93; on
    mentoring, 176
resilience, 8
resources: searching out, 74; shared,
    179–80
respect, 74
responsibility: fiscal, 58; personal, 14, 131
restaurants, 45–47
restructuring businesses, 48–49
retirement, 43
reverse mentoring, 104
Richard Caruso Mentoring Series, 161
Richard E. and Sally F. Caruso Mentor-
    ing and Innovation Center, 124–25,
    162–63
Rider University, 152
risk management, 45, 76, 96, 106–7, 123,
    148
Robbins, Jeff, x, 53–54, 84–85, 91, 135
Robbins, Pat, x, 54, 91, 135
Rodriguez, Jon, xii, 158
role models, 26, 40
roles, shifting, 80–81, 97, 179
Roy Rogers restaurants, 46
Rustler Steak Houses, xi, 45–48, 58–60,
    134–35

safety nets, 39
SAT/ACT, 154
satisfaction, personal, 35
Sauer, Shari, 144
saving money. See frugality
scholarships: academic, 26; athletic,
    14–15, 51–52
school bus stops, 55, 73
science, 12, 67, 85, 95, 99, 158–60
science, technology, engineering, and
    mathematics (STEM), 158–60

Seaview Country Club, 5, 44
Secretariat, 91
secretaries, personal, 48
SEEDCO Industrial Park, 124
seed funding, 150
Seeger, Diena, 150
self-assessment tools, 146
self-determination, 29, 80, 175
self-interest, networking and, 68
self-reliance, 77–78
Selinsgrove, Pennsylvania, 15, 23
sensory-stimulating training products,
    150
serial entrepreneurs, 45
Shabazz, Betty, 112
sharing: goals, 25, 170, 179; good feeling
    of, 7–8; power of, 97
shining shoes, 7–8, 161
ship leasing, 47
Shriners Burn Institute, 190
Shu Ching (Chinese Book of History), 141
Sicily, 3, 44
silicone, 98, 191
Sinatra, Frank, 6, 11, 22
Sizzler Steak House, 59
skating rinks, 134
skin, artificial, 97–112, 189–92
skin grafts, 98
skipping classes, 10–11
ski trips, 32–38, 69
Slattery, Frank, 34, 44, 138–39
Smart Personalized Medicine, 121
Smith, Fred, 34–35
smoking, 129
Smolinski, Jacob, xii, 161
soda manufacturing, 12
Solar Divide, 150–51
solutions, finding. See problem solving
Sorbonne University, 185
South Africa, 143
South America, 143
sparkle phase, 76–77
Special Achievement Award in Business
    and Health, NIAF, 126
specialty training workshops, 170
speeding tickets, 51

Squarespace, 151
Ss. Colman-John Neumann School, 159–60
stakeholders, interests of, 49
start-up ventures, 30–34, 69, 93–97, 100, 119, 152, 180
stealing hubcaps, 11
steering committees, 71, 169
Steese, Brad, 157
STEM. *See* science, technology, engineering, and mathematics (STEM)
Stevenson, Robert Louis, 140
stimulus, economic, 35
St. Joseph's University, 21, 24
St. Katharine of Siena School, 138, 158–59
St. Martin de Porres School, 159
St. Michael's School, 5, 9–10, 134
Stokes, Jessica, ix, 144
strategies, self-determination of, 29, 52
street smarts, 13, 105–6
strength through mentoring, 153
structured mentoring, 87–90, 141–47, 169–73, *173*
struggling, financial, 5
stubbornness, 43
success: definition of, 132; financial, 61, 167; individual determination of, 81; mentoring and, 81; multiple mentorships and, 80; personal, 60; of protégés, 90; wealth as measure of, 82
Sullivan, Jim, xi, 46–47, 59–60, 86, 135
summer jobs, 12–14
Summers, Monique, 145–46
support, culture of, 70
SurveyMonkey, 170
suspension from school, 17–18
Susquehanna University, 14, 17, 22–26, 120, 124, 131, 162
sustainability, 49–50
Sweden, 143
Swindoll, Charles, 183–84
Switzerland, 88
symposium, on mentoring, 67–68, 69, 87

talent, organizational, 148
talent search programs, 155
Tampa Bay Buccaneers, 23

tax laws, 53, 121
Tax Reform Act, 1986, 83
technology: leading-edge, 61, 93, 167; mentoring in, 158–60
Technology Mentoring Program (TMP), 158–60
Tech Titans after-school computer club, 159
Telemachus, 72, 80
telephone companies, 35–36
Telios Pharmaceuticals, 109–10
tenacity. *See* perseverance
Tenly Enterprises, 46, 59, 60
Texas, West, 72–73
Thailand, 88
theological education, 147
3-D printing, 158
Tiananmen Square, 88
TMP. *See* Technology Mentoring Program (TMP)
Tokyo, 88
Tomasso, Don, 46
Tonight Show, 122
top-down relationships, 69, 171
tough-guy persona, 52
town-improvement projects, 124
training, 69–71, 84
trains, 37, 48–49
transparency, 48
transplants, organ, 94
trust, 77, 105, 117, 130, 135–36
Turbo Train, 37
Turner, Ted, 35
Tyrell, Peter, x–xi, 10, 130, 135–36

UIF. *See* Uncommon Individual Foundation (UIF)
unassigned help, 89
uncertainty, 114
Uncommon Individual Award, 143–44
Uncommon Individual Foundation (UIF), 141–64; goals of, 81; growth of, 119–22, 141; meditation at offices, 126; naming of, 66; outreach programs, 133; process for, 71; research on mentoring, 78, 85–87; staff at, xii
Uncommon Man, The (Greenewalt), 63, 66

uniqueness, 64
United Aircraft, 37
United Kingdom, 143
University of Illinois, 189
University of Pennsylvania, 85
Upward Bound Program, 155
Urbas, Pamela, xi, 126

vacations, family, 57–58, 87–88
Valley Forge, Pennsylvania, 36
value systems, 88, 118
Venafro, Italy, 3
venture capital firms, 107, 120
videos: educational, 153–54; on
    mentoring, 161; production of, 160,
    163–64
Villanova, Pennsylvania, 52, 115, 135
Villanova University, 52
virtue, personal, 187
vision, creation of, 61, 102, 167

Wagenhein, Ronnie, x–xi, 10–11, 13, 121
Wall Street Journal, 64, 114
Waring, Laura, 157
Washington, DC, 37, 127

watching people, 130
Wayne, Pennsylvania, 158, 162
wealth: culture of, 22, 41, 58, 118; success
    measured by, 82; use of, 63
Weekly Fight, The, 163–64
West Chester, Pennsylvania, 157
West Point Military Academy, 20, 70
Wharton, 85
White House Sub Shop, 6
wills, administration of, 50, 63
Wilmington, Delaware, 29
win-win thinking, 49
work experience, 30, 152
Workshop Series, OnTrack, 152–53
wound care products, 109–10
Wynnewood, Pennsylvania, 38–39

X, Malcolm, 112

Yannas, Ioannis V., 97–100, 109, 189–94
Yannas, Vassilios, 190
yoga, 126
Youth Literacy Program, 152–57

Zivic, Andrew, xii, 15